101 Ways to Make

Your Classroom Special

Creating a place where significance, teamwork, and
spontaneity can sprout and flourish

James D. Sutton, Ed.D.
Illustrated by Timothy E. Wiegenstein

Friendly Oaks Publications
Pleasanton, TX 78064

Published by:
    Friendly Oaks Publications
    P.O. Box 662
    Pleasanton, TX 78064-0662 (USA)
    (830) 569-3586
    fax: (830) 281-2617

All rights reserved

Last digit is print number: 6 5 4 3 2

Library of Congress Cataloging-in-Publication Data

Sutton, James D.
    101 ways to make your classroom special: creating a place where
significance, teamwork, and spontaneity can sprout and flourish /
James D. Sutton; illustrated by Timothy E. Wiegenstein.
        p. 168 cm. 15x23
    ISBN 1-878878-57-3 (softcover)
    1. Teaching. 2. Teachers. 3. Classroom environment. 1. Title.
II. Title: One hundred one ways to make your classroom special.
III. Title: One hundred and one ways to make your classroom special.
LB1025.S88 1999
371.102--dc21   99-17478
                                                                       CIP

$11.95 Softcover

Consistent with the spirit of Activity #87, the author and Friendly Oaks Publications have set aside part of the proceeds from this book to sponsor needy children in Africa, Asia, and Latin America.

Other books by Dr. James D. Sutton:

If My Kid's So Nice ... Why's He Driving ME Crazy?
It Makes a Difference
Children of Crisis, Violence, and Loss
Windows

Dedication

This book is dedicated to all the youngsters who have passed through my life, and to the adults who have inspired them.

Teach from the Inside Out

Teach from the inside out on your journey each day.
Sing your own song in your own way.
Awaken, be real, let there be no doubt.
Say "Yes, I can! And yes, I will!"
Teach—from the inside out.

— Elizabeth Jeffries

"Teach from the Inside Out" was originally written and published by Elizabeth Jeffries and titled "Lead from the Inside Out." Adapted and printed with permission.

Table of Contents

Foreword

James Sutton has written another valuable book for educators. *101 Ways to Make Your Classroom Special* is a feast of ideas brimming with novelty and enjoyable activities. Through stories, examples, and strategies Jim engages the reader while addressing the critical need for students to feel they are citizens of their classrooms, not just visitors. Learning is optimal when students are alert and relaxed, when they feel ownership, and when they have good feelings about who and where they are. The suggestions Jim shares implement these fundamentals.

Jim has brought a wealth of expertise and ideas from his own classroom teaching, years of counseling, and the delivery of hundreds of staff development workshops in schools and universities across America. Educators shared those strategies they found successful. Many of them are in this book.

Jim exemplifies the power of positive relationships. His positive approaches and importance of fun in learning permeate his approach. Indeed, teachers across the country are moving from a focus on teaching to a focus on learning. *101 Ways to Make Your Classroom Special* is a valuable tool in this learning toolbox.

— Marvin Marshall, Ed.D.
How To Discipline without Rewards or Punishments
www.MarvinMarshall.com

A Great Teacher

The lesson

My first driving lesson almost killed me *and* my father.

I had a summer job working with Dad in the oilfields. On a slow day, we piled into the old Dodge for my first driving lesson. I lost control of the clutch, and we lurched into a collision course with a group of storage tanks. I panicked, my right foot stuck to the floor.

It was all over.

But Dad didn't panic. He cut the ignition and turned the wheel just enough to avoid a collision. We plowed safely into the sandy bank of a water pit.

He was not upset; I was. I vowed never again to occupy the driver's seat. I was done with it. Finished.

"What is this car doing right now?" Dad asked patiently. He sensed my panic.

"Uh—nothing, Dad. It's not doing anything."

"That's right. And it's not going to do anything. Unless you *make* something happen, this car will sit here until it's a pile of rust."

We continued the lesson. I not only learned how to drive that day, I learned two things that would follow me for life. I learned that my father, although not a professional educator, was a great teacher. I also learned that knowledge, confidence, and meaningful relationships are powerful antidotes for fear and doubt.

What better place?

Other than home, what better place is there for a youngster to learn these "antidotes" than at school? Although the sharing of some of these skills, ideas, and processes (antidotes) has been my purpose in writing this book, there certainly have been those times of self-examination. It's hard sometimes to look deeply into the mirror, but it can be the starting point of our greatest growth.

I made my share of mistakes as a teacher, especially as a new teacher. Even today it's tough coming to grips with the fact that, in my classroom experiences, I sometimes contributed more to problems than to their solutions. I made it a point to learn from those times and become better.

But I really doubt I am alone in confronting the downside of a healthy and serious self-look. In the business of serving young people we make mistakes; we fall short of the mark. Youngsters are gracious enough to forgive us a mistake or two, as long as they know that our *intent* carries the stamp of sterling. We can grow the most from just these kinds of experiences. Everyone benefits.

These pages contain contributions of some of the best educators in the profession. They in turn gained many of their ideas and activities from other teachers, friends, and mentors in the profession.

This book is for those who choose to accept the challenge of excellence. In doing so, they will surely make a difference.

Just one more ride ...

My father, Fred Sutton, passed away in the fall of 1998, about the time I was finishing the first draft of this book. The effects of his guidance in my life, however, continue.

Indeed, there are those times when I yearn to climb into the old Dodge for just one more ride with a great teacher.

Acknowledgments

Those teachers and school counselors who freely shared many of the ideas and activities discussed in this book deserve the credit and kudos for their input. As overworked as they may be, the words "Without them, this book would not have been possible" are absolutely true.

Tim Wiegenstein did more than illustrate this book with fabulous cartoons. He turned a project into a passion. Every single one of the four batches of artwork he sent me were so great that, whenever I opened one, my excitement about this project was ignited all over again.

My earlier book, *If My Kid's So Nice ... Why's He Driving ME Crazy?*, was a success much to the credit of bookcover artist and designer Robert Howard. He certainly has worked his magic again. Robert is quite old-fashioned in one important way: he cares deeply about making his client's product the very best it can be. I'm betting Robert's going to stay that way.

I am appreciative to master educators Dr. Marv Marshall and Dr. Harry Wong. Their support and encouragement through letters, phone calls, e-mail, and comments about this book were a welcomed source of help and encouragement.

Thanks also to Anne Hebenstreit for her diligent copy editing and proofreading of this work. Anne performed a very critical service and did it well, especially when she faced some pretty tight deadlines as the manuscript reached its final form.

And, as always, I am thankful to my family. They have been a driving force not only behind this book, but in my life as well.

Chapter One

The Challenge

"Stay away ..."

"Stay away from negative people."

I turned to check out the source of that piece of advice. It came from the teacher across the hall from my classroom. She was a veteran of many years.

"I'm serious," she said, pointing down the hall.

My gaze followed her gesture—to the door of the faculty lounge. Pretty interesting stuff to encounter your first week on the job.

Although I didn't really absorb all she told me right away, before long I had figured out that there *were* a few folks in that school who were just hanging around for a paycheck and a summer vacation. She never exactly spelled it out to me, but I concluded that my mentor was referring to the element of cynicism that can be found in just about *all* professions.

Of course bouts of "brown-out" (a temporary, nonfatal case of burn-out) can infect any of us, especially when we're tired. Teaching is rigorous and demanding. It's a challenge that exacts its share of wear and tear to the point of walking, talking exhaustion. Fortunately, such teachers can, and do, recover.

Been there; done that.

Wanted: a goat

But cynicism is different. It's a deadly poison. Cynics are not interested in solutions; they just look to lay blame for their shortcomings. They endure (painfully so for the rest of us), but they rarely change. They look for a goat, and any goat will do. Listen to them:

> *These kids today just don't appreciate anything you do for them.*

> *They never care about learning anything.*

> *They're just rude, rude, rude—that's all.*

> *Don't worry about doing a good job around here; no one cares anyway.*

There's danger sandwiched between these one-size-fits-all perspectives. They all fail to recognize that one can *still* find committed teachers, involved students, and supportive parents.

If you don't believe this is true, you've picked up the wrong book.

Fundamentals

Be plenty careful if anyone attempts to sell you a new fundamental. There aren't any. Fundamentals are incredibly stable, valuable, and consistent over time. And they are not at all difficult to understand (which, I'm sure, is why they can cause us such trouble). The subtitle of this book, *Creating a place where significance, teamwork, and spontaneity can sprout and flourish*, addresses three such fundamentals. Although I have encountered these fundamentals many times in my work as an educator and a child and adolescent psychologist, I fully realize they apply to adults every bit as much as they do to young people. Let's take a closer look at them:

12

Fundamental #1: Everyone wants to feel significant

No one wants to just take up space on the planet. They want to feel that they matter, and that they are capable of being affirmed. Remember Jaime Escalante, the teacher who succeeded in taking a group of average youngsters from Garfield High School in Los Angeles to incredible heights in mathematics? The movie *Stand and Deliver* portrayed his accomplishments, which led to his being recognized as Teacher of the Year. He helped his students feel significant, and the rest is history.

I provide counseling to youngsters at a prominent children's home in south Texas. One day I was standing in front of the administration building as the school bus brought the youngsters home. Several of them saw me and immediately captured my attention, pointing to themselves ("Send for me, send for me"). They wanted to spend some time with me because it made them feel significant. It goes without saying that I deeply value their corresponding affirmation of me. The day when there are no youngsters on that bus wanting to see me is the day I step down from serving children—with or without the gold watch.

Significance is closely tied to one's ability to self-affirm. Most youngsters sense whether they feel significant or not, even if they have difficulty expressing it. And it is exactly here, in the expression of feelings of significance (or difficulties with it), where we can be of great service. I am tempted to say, "where we can be of tremendous service." It is that important.

Significance and self-affirmation enhance one's ability to self-soothe. Although it's important that we comfort and soothe others in their times of need, we *must* be able to soothe ourselves. When no one else is around to comfort us, it helps to be able to say, "I'm okay. Even though things are temporarily falling apart around me, *I'm* okay." In other words, the ability to self-soothe is the skill of emotional self-repair. Much is tied to this one aspect of significance.

And, of course, significance comes right back to achievement. This includes not only academic success in school, but the ability to exercise initiative and take healthy risks toward achievement, especially when a challenge is difficult (more will be said about initiative and risk-taking in chapter six).

Youngsters run on the fuel of significance, and teachers bring the spark that ignites them to action. Indeed, many of the ideas and activities in this book focus on this one very powerful fundamental—significance.

Fundamental #2: We must learn to live and work with one another

We do not live in a vacuum. Everything and everyone are connected in some way. Positively or negatively, one person's wants and actions *always* affect others. Dennis Prager's provocative book *Happiness Is a Serious Problem* suggests that a person who is always committed to securing their own happiness will become both selfish and miserable. Perhaps this is one reason that the majority of first marriages in this country end in divorce.

Awareness not only of the presence of others, but of the *need* for others is critical for all of us, but it is especially critical for our children. Many of the ideas and activities in this book focus on work teams (such as Cooperative Learning groups), group problem-solving, and the development of sensitivity toward others and the environment.

Fundamental #3: Life is meant to be enjoyed, not simply endured

Have you ever asked someone, "How are you doing?" and got the reply, "Oh, I guess I'll make it." Would you want that person teaching *your* kids or grandchildren—someone who was only *making it*?

14

Life is not to be tolerated or endured, but rather taken in large gulps. It's not intended to be a gauntlet where the goal is to make it to the end semi-alive. Sure, life is tough sometimes, but that's no reason to plant ourselves in the same piece of poisoned ground where the cynics grow.

Spontaneity and the enjoyment of life can be summarized in one word: *fun*. The ability to have fun is unrehearsed, therefore spontaneous. But we all have encountered youngsters who have not had any fun in years. They don't even recognize it when it's right in front of them. (My wife Bobbie still recalls taking her whole class to a rodeo, where, right in the middle of the whole experience, a student turned to her and asked, "Are we having fun yet?")

"ARE YOU MARRIED ?!"

Spontaneity is so important that, when I do assessments with youngsters, I'm apt to ask a six-year-old, "Are you married?" Now there's generally only one answer to that question, right? But I am sensitive as to how the child responds to it. If the youngster looks at me in wide-eyed amazement like I just lost my mind, or begins to laugh like it's the funniest thing they ever heard, I am encouraged. If, on the other hand, a child simply answers my question with no change in affect or expression, I'm concerned.

Spontaneity can and should be found everywhere: homes, classrooms, weddings—even funerals.

I'm sometimes asked to explain the difference between spontaneity and impulsivity. Simple. Spontaneity comes from a good place within a person, creating a perspective of, "This is the right thing to do, and this is the right time and place to do it." Almost always, spontaneous acts are constructive, kind, and beneficial. Impulsivity, on the other hand, comes from need, creating a perspective of, "I've got to do this or I'm going to explode." Impulsive acts are usually destructive, and they take a toll on relationships.

Risk-taking and spontaneity are linked. The ability to take a healthy, productive risk relies heavily upon spontaneity (and, of course, the positive sense of self that fosters spontaneity).

I saw an excellent example of this connection between risk-taking and spontaneity once when I attended a graduation lunch for a small group of 12th-graders. Prizes were being awarded, and one young man won a hat—a very tall, comic hat. It was obvious that he was embarrassed about the prize as he claimed it and walked back to his seat. Everyone in the room asked him to try it on, but he wouldn't. The more they insisted, the more he refused, and the more embarrassed he became.

Finally, one of his friends reached for the hat, put it on his own head, and wore it for the rest of the party. I later learned that the friend who wore the silly hat was an honor student, a natural leader, and a gifted athlete.

No coincidence. There are ideas and activities in this book that will help you foster spontaneity and risk-taking ability in young people.

And, oh yes, one last piece of advice: Stay away from negative people.

Dennis Prager's book *Happiness Is a Serious Problem* is published by HarperCollins (1998).

Chapter Two

Using This Book

These ideas and activities address many skills and competencies for the school, the classroom, and life. They encourage thinking and acting, without necessarily suggesting a "correct" answer. Creativity is always encouraged. Teach youngsters to value it. In the words of Charles Kettering: "The opportunities of man are limited only by his imagination. But so few have imagination that there are ten thousand fiddlers to one composer."

Hey, there's nothing wrong with bringing along a composer or two in your professional lifetime.

A *lot* of help

The material here has been collected through my contact with educators over the past ten years or so. Without their help, there would be no book. I picked up many of these ideas and activities while conducting training for teachers and other child service professionals at over three dozen universities nationwide. Wherever possible, I have gone back to these folks, acknowledged their contribution, and asked for their permission to include it in this book. I have given them credit; this is only right.

There were other times, however, when ideas were shared in a rapidly moving session of training. Bear in mind that I was collecting successful ideas and activities long before this book was even a thought. Sometimes I captured an idea, activity, or strategy, but failed to get a name or a reference for it. In these instances where I have included an idea or activity that I *know* is not mine, I have attempted to at least identify *where* I collected it. Anyone recognizing their contributions here need only contact me to be acknowledged when the book is revised or reprinted.

As I travel the country working with many educators, counselors, and child service professionals, I am aware that there are a lot of folks doing creative and productive things with young people. Had I tried to include them all (a thoroughly impossible task), I'm afraid that this book would never have been printed in the first place.

Tips on using this book

Tip #1: Make ideas and intent congruent

Always think, "Who will benefit the most from this idea or activity?" The answer should be: "The students." But it's a great question to keep asking, as it brings focus. (As Zig Ziglar is fond of saying, "The *main* thing is to keep the *main* thing—the *main* thing!")

Why do I mention something that seems so obvious? Because it's too easy to slip into some of these ideas and activities as a convenience to ourselves. If this happens too often, effectiveness will be lost. Youngsters can tolerate, and even appreciate, a maneuver that redirects them to task, but no one likes to be served a main course of what they see as a bag of tricks.

Tip #2: Incorporate what will work for you

It would be great if every single page of this book were a gold mine for you. Great, but not realistic. Some ideas and activities either will not work at all in some cases, or they will require too much time and resources to implement.

For instance, one activity in chapter three suggests asking parents for a letter of introduction to their son or daughter. If you happened to know that folks living near your school might struggle with reading and writing, you probably wouldn't use that idea at all, or would modify it (such as an interview with parents in the evening by phone).

Tip #3: Always think spin-off

Sometimes one idea will trigger another one or remind you of something that you might have used in the past. Keep spinning off and 101 ways can become 201.

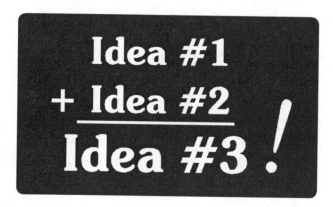

Tip #4: Combine and cross-apply

Consider combining and recombining groups of ideas and activities. For example, chapter six introduces the activity of brainstorming, while activity #29 in chapter four has youngsters generating feelings cards to use with other exercises in that chapter. Here we have a practical application of the activity of brainstorming. Activities #8 and #73 involve magic tricks, demonstrating that a skill, once learned, can be used for several purposes. There are other similar opportunities in this book.

Tip #5: Modify for age of students

At first glance some of these ideas and activities might seem inappropriate for the age of your students. With some modification, however, many will still work. For example, the idea of putting an Origami bird on a student's desk (#7) could be modified to fit an older student. Instead of an actual paper sculpture, put an envelope containing instructions and some paper on the desk instead (perhaps with a note like, "Can you show me how to make this?").

Tip #6: Encourage group processing

Cooperative Learning has stayed around for a good reason. Teaching youngsters to work together in groups pays off in so many ways.

Chapter Three

A Teacher's Touch

"Daddy, you're a teacher?" my three-year-old asked, his voice brimming with adoration. I had just shared with my wife the telephone script I had been using. That evening teachers from my school had been working the phone bank for a gubernatorial candidate.

To my son, nothing could top a teacher. Nothing.

Teachers have an opportunity to touch the lives of young people in ways that other adults cannot. Every variable is on the teacher's side: relationship, time, and purpose. The opportunity exists for teacher-youngster relationships at all age categories.

The very young are likely to project their preconceived ideas, thoughts, and judgments about adults onto every new adult they encounter. Some children see adults as warm and nurturing toward children. It's no chore at all to have a good year with the youngster who's "prewired" for it.

On the other hand, what if a child views adults as being impatient, unreasonable, demanding, hard, and punitive? This youngster is apt to think, "Well, here's another one." And they will behave accordingly. Such an attitude can mean big trouble from day one.

Such a child is not necessarily planning or intending to be "bad." The youngster is simply following a familiar script that

22

provides an identity. It might not be a pleasant identity, or even one the child chooses, but it *is* an identity. It's like the old adage, "Halitosis is better than no breath at all!" Think about it; many behavioral problems of youngsters happen when the teacher accepts the child's bad script rather than attempting to improve it.

Then there are students (usually older ones) who have figured out that not all adults are like Mom or Dad, and they have adjusted their behavior accordingly. I worked with one adolescent girl who lived in a group home. Her mother and father were totally dysfunctional, both absolutely consumed by drug and alcohol addiction. Their lives cycled through rehabilitation centers, jails, and hospitals. But this girl was wise enough to move on with her life, realizing that it was best not to wait for her folks to change. She is in Gifted and Talented classes, and well on her way to earning full scholarships upon graduation from high school.

It was interesting to listen to this bright girl talk about her teachers. She did not project her parents' behaviors onto them. But she did share that many of her teachers seemed to be just going through the motions, having lost much of their zest for the profession. "Oh, they're showing up every day," she told me, "but it's like their pilot lights snuffed out some time ago."

And we don't think they notice? Youngsters today need to be taught, that's for sure. But they are also starving to be touched, touched in a way that revives their spirits and re-energizes them to learn and perform at their peak. At the same time, they need to experience the qualities of spontaneity and reasonableness. And what better way to learn these lessons than from teachers who make quality of life as high a priority as subject matter?

Here are 28 ideas and activities for extending a *teacher's touch*. Select a few that fit your personality, style, and circumstances, then give them a try.

#1

Doorway "Wonging"

Here's one I learned from Dr. Harry Wong, popular educator and trainer. Harry was a year or two ahead of me in the doctoral program at Brigham Young University (and I'm Baptist; go figure). One summer he spoke to our group, and my view of young people has been different ever since.

Harry shared a simple strategy he performed every day with every class, and it paid off immensely. Harry observed that he was faithful to this ritual, and it made his whole school year not only easier, but fun.

Harry would stand at the door to his junior high classroom and personally greet every student with a smile and a touch—a handshake. (Note: Touching students is a delicate issue today. It must be handled carefully and with sensitivity. If the youngster is uncomfortable with touch, or if your school or district has implemented a policy against touching students, don't do it. This being said, I'm convinced that there are plenty of youngsters who are starving for this simple gesture.)

Doorway greetings work! Check out your local Wal-Mart store. There's always someone at the door to greet you as you enter. From the beginning, Sam Walton knew he could take this gesture of personal interest all the way to the bank.

One final thought regarding touch: youngsters will give you clues. I was working with a seven-year-old at a children's home. When it was time for her to leave, she walked to the door, then abruptly turned and ran back into my office. She literally launched herself at me, hugging me tightly around the neck. With no need for words she said to me, "It's okay."

Thanks to Harry for granting permission for me to share this story and use the term and concept of "Wonging." He and his wife, Rosemary, make their home in Sunnyvale, California.

#2

Seated "Wonging"

One teacher shared how she has been "Wonging" her students for years, but with a different twist. Since she has a small group, a self-contained classroom, she "Wongs" youngsters at their desks.

The teacher writes each student's name on a popsicle stick and places all of the sticks in a skirt pocket. She then makes it a point to affirm each youngster whose name is in her pocket, moving the corresponding stick to the other pocket. By the end of the day, all of the sticks have been transferred, ensuring that she has made an attempt to affirm each student in a positive, personal, and special way.

Obviously it's important that this affirmation not become mechanical. The sticks are simply a guide, a reminder to the teacher. The students shouldn't even know about them.

I picked up this idea years ago. Unfortunately, I do not have the name of the teacher who shared it.

#3

Remedial "Wonging"

Remedial "Wonging" is similar to the other "Wongings," except that it singles out specific youngsters for additional affirmation. This method is especially recommended for youngsters who project poor self-concept or those students who tend to be oppositional and noncompliant.

It is very important to keep this special "Wonging" short, no more than 30 seconds or so. If it goes on longer than that, it becomes too obvious and will lose its effectiveness (don't we all like to be affirmed by those who recognize us spontaneously, and not out of obligation?). It's also important to keep these affirmations short because instructional time is always at a premium.

The subtle message with this sort of "Wonging" is: "I really *do* care about you. I want to be fair and reasonable, and recognize you as a person." This gesture serves to separate you from the tasks you assign, and represents a brief focus on a relationship rather than an output.

Initially the effect of this approach is temporary. Over time, however, the relationship improves, as does task completion. My book *If My Kid's So Nice ... Why's He Driving ME Crazy?* offers more insight and strategies for working specifically with oppositional and defiant youngsters.

If My Kid's So Nice ... Why's He Driving ME Crazy? is published by Friendly Oaks Publications (1997).

#4

A note from the teacher

I suppose you could call this one printed "Wonging." Focus only on four or five students per day, with a plan to affirm every youngster in the classroom at least once during the week.

Write a supportive line or two to each student, making it specific to that child. Place the note in an envelope and seal it. Write the youngster's name on the envelope, and place it on the student's desk before the class arrives.

This is a powerful strategy because there is no need for you to say anything. You've already said it. Frankly, we talk too much anyway. If a child chooses to say something to you about the note, that's fine. If not, that's fine also. Just observe the youngster's subsequent behaviors. Over time they should speak volumes.

I believe what makes this particular activity so powerful is that a written note is both personal and permanent. A note, unlike a spoken word, can be read and re-read. Limiting these written notes to just a few youngsters at a time keeps them special. If you wrote notes for every student on the same day, it wouldn't mean as much.

Let me share a brief story to emphasize the value of this idea. I worked with one girl who lived in a group home. Her mother was under psychiatric care and was unable to raise her. Whenever the girl went home for a visit, the roles always reversed: the daughter took care of the mother.

When the girl moved into the group home, she was upset. Her behavior showed it. But she did have strong self-esteem and excellent leadership abilities. I came to the facility early one morning, and I wrote her a brief letter explaining the many qualities I saw in her. I wrote that she had the skills and ability to make a difference not only in her life, but in the lives of others.

She was deeply touched by the letter, the unit staff told me, although she *never* said a word to me about it. She showed the letter to her case worker and the staff, and even took it to a placement meeting, where she showed it to everyone in attendance.

But she never mentioned it to me. No matter; it worked.

#5

"Posted"

Instead of a letter or note in an envelope, try writing an affirmation down on a Post-It note. Deliver it during seatwork activities. Perhaps you don't have to write anything; a happy face, or even a big "check plus," would do.

In order to make this activity more meaningful, limit the number of notes that you write at any given time or day.

One teacher shared with me that he writes notes to his youngsters on those "While You Were Out" message pads. Benefit: he retains a copy of the note, which can prove helpful later. He indicated that this kind of note is also excellent for silently redirecting a youngster to task.

The "While You Were Out" message pad idea was shared by a high school teacher from New York State when I presented a program for the Capital Area School Development Association. Sorry, I did not get his name.

#6

A little balloony

Buy a package of those long, thin balloons that are used to make balloon sculptures of different animals. Many gift or novelty shops carry these, along with books of instructions for beginners on making simple balloon sculptures. These balloons can be hard to inflate until you get the hang of it, so consider buying a small pump too. Memorize five or six of the most common designs so you can leave a different animal on the desk of each of several children. Be certain to write the child's name on each balloon with a permanent marker. This will make it more special to the child, and it will reduce conflict.

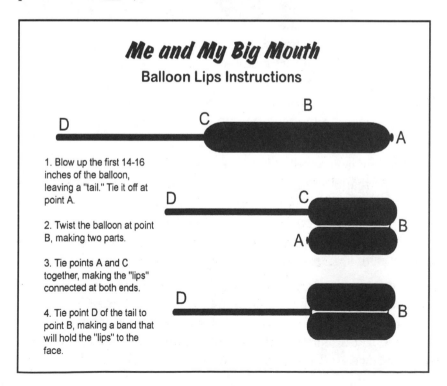

Me and My Big Mouth
Balloon Lips Instructions

1. Blow up the first 14-16 inches of the balloon, leaving a "tail." Tie it off at point A.

2. Twist the balloon at point B, making two parts.

3. Tie points A and C together, making the "lips" connected at both ends.

4. Tie point D of the tail to point B, making a band that will hold the "lips" to the face.

Included here are the instructions for one of my favorites. I call it "Me and My Big Mouth." The first time you make these balloon lips, put them on and model them for the class (they also double as a cool pair of sunglasses). If this creation doesn't bring a reaction, better check for a pulse. *Every* kid will want a pair of these.

#7

Origami

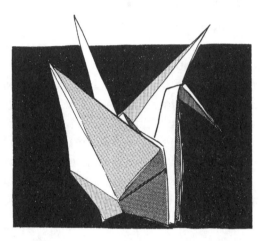

Origami is the Japanese art of paper folding, a type of sculpture. When I saw youngsters in private therapy, I would often take a sheet of paper and turn it into a crane (the traditional and most popular design), a frog, or some other animal. Kids absolutely loved them, especially when I wrote their names on my creations. Try making a few of these designs, then leave them on the desks of students as you would the notes or balloons. Don't say anything about it, or even where they came from. Let them figure it out.

Just about any city library has at least one book on making simple Origami designs. Type in "Origami" on an Internet search engine, and you will be directed to a number of free sites that can teach you how to create designs. Beginning designs are not all that difficult, they're easy to memorize, and they have lasting impact with students and one's own children and grandkids.

I even found one Internet site that shows how to make Origami out of dollar bills (type "Money Origami" into your search engine). I checked out this site, and it is great! I made a shirt from a dollar in just a couple of minutes. The site has all kinds of neat stuff that can be made from a dollar bill (boat, boot, shirt, ring, spider, eyeglasses, and other things). The author of the web site said that he leaves these little sculptures as tips in restaurants. As a result he always gets great service when he returns.

Now, actually making sculptures out of dollar bills for your students could get expensive (I suppose you could make them from dollar-bill-sized pieces of paper, but that wouldn't be any fun), but it *will* get their attention. If you are collecting money from students and need to make change, try handing a youngster one of these designs that you have already made.

For older students, try putting some instructions and a few sheets of folding paper or a dollar bill in an envelope with this note: "I tried to make this, and couldn't do it. Can you figure it out—and teach me?" This is relationship-building because the youngster is now in a position to help you, and must take the initiative to approach you since you are not going to say any more about it. Besides, if the child doesn't do it, what have you lost?

#8

Magic!

All youngsters love magic tricks, especially if they can learn to do them also. Simple tricks are the best, especially those tricks that use stuff kids can find around the house, like string, rope, paper clips, coins, and playing cards. The school library  should have a book or two on magic tricks. Practice them until you can do them easily.

Introduce students to the fun of magic, then follow up by putting a description of a trick on a child's desk. Challenge them to show you they can perform it. See some ways that this can be turned into a language arts activity?

#9

Candlelight luncheon

An elementary school teacher shared how she would extend an invitation to a couple of youngsters to join her in the classroom for a candlelight luncheon. She regularly invited youngsters to this luncheon on a rotating basis. She would set up a card table, drape it with a tablecloth, and add a pair of real candlesticks.

The lunch itself was usually simple, perhaps just fruit, cheese, and crackers, but it was always a memorable event to the students. Youngsters eagerly waited to receive their invitation in the mail, which meant that the parents were aware of the luncheon.

If you try this idea, add an RSVP line to the invitation just to make it interesting. See what happens.

Unfortunately, I don't have the name of the teacher who shared this great idea.

#10

Invitation to tea

Here is a similar activity for after lunch. It's a tea ceremony with youngsters teaching each other the ritual of serving. It is an excellent vehicle for oral language development and the practice of social skills.

It's like a tea chain letter, and it works like this: The teacher invites one child to tea immediately after lunch while the rest of the students are at recess. The child is taught how to boil the water, prepare the tea, pour it, and clean up afterward. Thereafter, that child prepares tea for another youngster, teaching them the process, and so on.

One word of caution: Since there is potential danger with boiling water, an adult always needs to be near.

Here's another borrowed idea I cannot connect with a name.

#11

Special time

The person who shared this idea noted that it had a profoundly positive effect on her life. She related how one of her teachers in elementary school would offer to stay after school for 30 minutes each day in order to visit with every student on a rotating basis.

Apparently there was no set agenda. He was all ears to whatever *they* wanted to talk about. These visits helped her to put early family difficulties into perspective and encouraged her to take the initiative to make some changes.

Nothing is more affirming than our presence and a noncritical ear.

This idea was shared by Lissie Brooks, a social worker from Hartford, Connecticut.

#12

Dinner at your house

A teacher shared how she would pick one Saturday evening a month to host a dinner for her students.

No, not all of them at once. She broke the class into groups of four to five youngsters (Cooperative Learning groups might work well for this). They all received an invitation in the mail, with an RSVP line.

When the students arrived, she would assign each of them a small task, such as putting ice in the glasses, preparing a salad, or setting the table. Everyone helped. After dinner they would play some games or perhaps watch a video.

For a creative twist on this idea, consider preparing a churn of homemade ice cream, letting the youngsters take turns handcranking their dessert.

This idea was shared with me during a program at the University of Arizona in Tucson. I don't have a name.

#13

Home visits

Now this one is really different. Turn a parent conference into a housecall? Absolutely. Sometimes you might be able to arrange to meet a parent at their place of work. It might be a bit difficult to achieve, but if you can schedule even one conference like this during the school year, it will have impact.

After a few years of teaching, the remainder of my school experience was spent doing assessments with youngsters referred for Special Education placement and programming. As I would complete the testing, it was my responsibility to set up the IEP (Individualized Education Plan) meetings. These meetings determined whether a youngster was eligible to receive Special Education services, and, if so, exactly how those services were to be structured and delivered. Any child already in Special Education was reviewed annually at a similar meeting. (During my last year in the public schools I conducted 223 of these meetings; that's why it was my *last* year.)

One such annual meeting was always a special treat for me. The child's guardian was his great-grandmother. Her fragile health made it difficult for her to travel to the school, so the principal, the school counselor, a couple of teachers, and I took the meeting to her house. What a treat; she made the best peanut butter cookies in the county.

#14

Signage

Put a small sign like this one above the door going *out* of your classroom:

Through these doors pass the _____ students of (name of school).

Every few days, change the word in the blank. Words could include:

kindest
most considerate
hardest working
most helpful
best team member
most enthusiastic

Deliberately keep this sign small and inconspicuous. Don't say anything about it at all; sometimes less really is more. Youngsters will find it eventually, and they will tell others.

Avoid words like "smartest" or "most attractive." Need some help with the words? After the youngsters capture the concepts of what you are doing with the sign, let them brainstorm other words for you (see #79 in chapter six). You might even let your Cooperative Learning groups take turns putting the words up each day for a week.

#15

Check the paper

Whenever a student gets some positive press in the local newspaper, clip the article (and photograph also, if there is one), and give it to the child in an envelope with a card which reads:

I saw this in the paper.
I'm glad I found it too.
It pleases me to be your teacher,
and to be so proud of you.

Just place it on their desk, no explanation or additional comment. (There is a possible downside to this little passage. Some youngsters might perceive that the reason for them to do well and to achieve is to please you or their parents, rather than *intrinsically* being pleased. If you feel this might be the case, you might try changing the last two lines.)

An elderly member of our church regularly combs the papers for news and photographs about folks she knows. On any given Sunday, she is apt to have a whole handful of clippings to pass out.

Coming from a teacher, this gesture can make a tremendous difference, not only with the child, but with the parents as well. Remember when you had your picture in the newspaper as a youngster? Your parents went out and bought a dozen or so copies of the paper, just so they could clip that one little piece and send it to relatives. Giving a clipping to the child can save the parents time and money.

#16

Send a card

Children typically don't get much mail. When they do, it is an event. My son Jamie once got an advertisement for a children's magazine when he was about four. It was bulk rate mail, but when I handed it to him, he lit up like a Christmas tree.

It's true; a quick postcard or a seasonal card is bound to be appreciated. I would recommend a seasonal card other than Christmas ones, simply because so many cards are sent and received then. Harvest cards in the fall can be sent around Halloween or Thanksgiving, as well as late winter and spring cards for the second semester. There are now excellent computer programs that can help you to make great cards quickly and inexpensively.

If you or someone you know is artistic, create your own artwork for these cards. These drawings can be scanned into the computer for use with future classes.

#17

"I thought of you" memento

When I travel, and I do quite a lot of it, I take a camera. (Hint: If you carry a camera, use it!) On a trip to California, I took a picture of the university extension center where I spoke. I mounted the photo in a small, inexpensive frame, and sent it to the dean. In less than two weeks I received a very warm letter of appreciation. This kind of goodwill can pay off in so many ways, but mostly it's just a nice thing to do.

When you are away from a youngster or a group of youngsters, and you remember them with a photograph, a postcard, or an inexpensive souvenir, it conveys a powerful message: "While I was away, I thought of *you*." This is a powerful gesture because those thoughts of the youngsters came when they were *not* in your presence. Everyone likes to be remembered, and this is a special and effective way to do it.

#18

Attend events

If you have an opportunity to attend an event featuring one of your students (such as choir, drama, or athletics), work on a way to let the youngster know you were there. This acknowledgment works well whether you share it verbally or in writing. Be certain to remark on something specific that the youngster did at the event. This lets him or her know that you really *were* there, and that you were paying attention.

#19

The "Gran Stand"

Grandparents have time for kids (isn't it ironic how we have more time as we grow older?). Unfortunately, with today's highly mobile society, a child's grandparents can be far away. So how about some "stand-in" grandparents at school?

Now the logistics would have to be worked out, but basically we're talking about one or two senior citizens who fill in as classroom grandparents to the students.

These folks could help with homework or assignments, or they could just sit at a "Gran Stand" in the back of the room and be available to visit and chat with youngsters who have finished their work. They could listen to youngsters read, and perhaps even bring a batch of cookies. This idea has a lot of possibilities.

With some slight modifications, I can easily see how this idea could be adapted for older students. Many youngsters today do not have access to older adults, and yet it is often older adults (who are not parents, teachers, or principals) who can develop a close and meaningful relationship with a tough-to-reach youngster.

#20

Lunch buddies

This suggestion is a spin-off of the Gran Stand. Encourage the classroom grandparents to eat with youngsters in the cafeteria. Eventually they might have to start carrying the lunchroom equivalent to a dance card.

If you are considering the development of a mentor program in your school, invite community leaders and business folks to stop by the school to have lunch with their mentee or a group of students. This is usually by appointment, so the students will know when their mentor is coming to lunch with them. I have eaten with youngsters at school in this manner and have *always* seen positive results. This can be a very positive way to brighten the lives of all those involved. Besides, there's something about breaking bread together that builds instant rapport.

#21

Jokes and stories

Kids of all ages love a good joke or story. In fact, it has been proven that, when important facts are supported by a story, retention is higher.

A joke or a story could be shared by the teacher, but I always enjoyed assigning a joke or a story to a student. I would tell them that they could get help from their classmates or their family, but they were responsible to share something the next day with the class.

This little activity reinforces the notion that you the teacher enjoy a good laugh, and that things do not have to be *totally* serious all of the time. Spontaneity is a critical attribute of humans, and humor is a critical component of spontaneity.

Without saying it in words, this little activity also teaches a measure of tolerance. Think about it; the child who fails to find a classmate's joke funny might have a little difficulty getting a response when their own turn comes.

#22

Hobbies and interests

Here's an excellent way to get your "Wonging" material. Give your students a questionnaire early in the school year. Ask about interests, hobbies, favorite activities, food preferences, and such. Included here is "My Favorite ... ," a sample questionnaire.

My Favorite ...

food:

color:

book:

sport:

hero:

subject in school:

hobby:

music:

vacation:

TV program:

things to collect:

pet:

things to do with my family:

Name:
Date:

Sample of a student questionnaire

My Child ...

is really good at:

loves to talk about:

is most frustrated when:

likes the school subjects of:

is a little shy about:

would like you to know that:

finds it difficult to:

works hardest when:

really enjoys:

is very proud of:

can be most helpful when:

Child's name:
Parent's name:
Date:

Sample of a parent questionnaire

#23

Parent questionnaire

How about a questionnaire for parents? In it you could ask for information about their child, as well as tips about important things they might want you to know. Also ask about any special talents or hobbies that the parents have, things you might be able to showcase to the class sometime during the school year.

#24

Letter of introduction

Here is an idea that is not for every situation, but it could be very interesting. Encourage parents to write you a letter of introduction for their child. Here's an example:

> **Dear Parents:**
> **It will be my pleasure to be Mary's teacher this school year. I look forward to having her in my class.**
> **Would you please consider writing me a letter of introduction for Mary?**
>
> **Thank you,**
> **Mary's teacher**

Although this simple note looks somewhat vague (it is!), it certainly allows parents to be creative and share what is uppermost in their minds. Also, since occasional strife is common in all families, this exercise usually encourages a parent to focus on the more positive attributes of their son or daughter.

#25

Baby picture roundup

Encourage all parents to loan you a baby picture of their child (without the child knowing about it). Put all of the students' baby pictures on a bulletin board, numbering each one. See which student can identify the most pictures. Make it a contest; offer a prize for the best job of pairing students up with their baby pictures.

#26

Hands around the school

Here's an idea that has tremendous impact on school and home, and it is easy to do. Ask every student to take home some construction paper and trace the hands of all the family members. The student then cuts them out and brings them back to school.

The "hands" are then taped at the top of the hallways, starting at the front door of the school and all the way around and back to the front.

I have seen this, and it is impressive. What an excellent way to visually present the message that everyone is "lending a hand." Why, some youngsters even traced the paws of their pets, bringing their "hands" to school also. Creative.

I saw this idea in action at Esparza Elementary School in San Antonio, Texas. The principal was Melva Matkin.

#27

Classroom notepads

Here's an easy activity that can instantly become quite a hit. Design a classroom notepad and provide it to the students.

Using a computer or the old-fashioned pen and ink, design the notepad to be the size of a quarter of a sheet of paper. This makes it easy for you to run them four up on the copier, then cut them into fourths. Make the last sheet of each notepad a piece of cardboard to make the notepad sturdy. Add a few blank pages between the pads, so it will be easy to separate them without wasting the custom pages. Pad them using white glue, putting weight on them until the glue dries. We've included a sample here that is close to actual size (actual size would be 4.25"x5.5").

Mrs. Blackburn's History Class

Sidell Avenue Intermediate School
Anywhere, USA

Be creative. You could change the notepads with the seasons and holidays. And if you want to teach a lesson in recycling, run the notepads on the backs of used paper. Also, if you are using Cooperative Learning groups, or other kinds of groups, consider customizing the notepads for each group.

#28

Appreciation certificate

Here's yet another kind of "Wonging." Everyone loves to be appreciated. Develop a small certificate of recognition simply to let a youngster know that you noticed their kindness in helping a new student learn their way around the school, take a frightened puppy to the office when it wandered into the school, or offered to help a classmate with an assignment they did not understand.

Sometimes it might be helpful to put these little certificates in envelopes so that they will be private, because some youngsters might be embarrassed even when recognized for a good deed.

Certificates for students are certainly not a new idea. The whole point, however, is how youngsters respond to them.

Appreciation Certificate

_____

is hereby recognized for
special consideration because:

_____   _____
Teacher's signature   Date

Chapter Four

Understanding Ourselves and Others

Needs: who needs them?

Here's an activity that focuses specifically on seven needs: *security, order, belonging, approval, worth, stimulation,* and *growth*. Obviously there are considerably more than seven needs, but these contain the essentials. Besides, youngsters can remember all or most of the seven, but they'd be lost with twenty-seven.

Go down the list of needs with your youngsters as you do some brainstorming with them (refer to activity #79 for instructions on brainstorming). Ask the students to explain what these needs mean to them, and provide some specific examples of each. This description should help:

The need for security:

The need for *security* is met by the basics like food, clothing, shelter, and protection in place. Security is associated with physical safety.

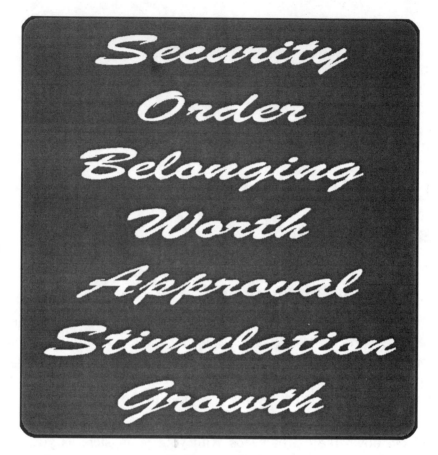

Needs

The need for order:

Order establishes the progression of circumstances and events. For instance, we eat breakfast before we eat lunch. For most of us order doesn't change much. Every day at school a youngster goes to math class before she goes to reading. Order implies predictability, which is a psychological form of security.

The need for belonging:

Belonging is the sense of "connectedness" to others. A family unit would be an example, although individuals can experience belonging at church, at work, in clubs, and at school.

The need for approval:

Approval is a pat on the back; it is affirmation. Although a paycheck is one form of affirmation, most people desire more than a paycheck. They want to be told that their work matters, and that they do it well.

The need for worth:

Worth is one's internal sense of self-value. People achieve worth when they are regarded and treated as being worthy.

The need for stimulation:

Stimulation fills our needs for something to do, as in a job or task, activity, plan, or "mission."

The need for growth:

The ongoing improvement pertains to all areas of a person's life, including intellectual, social, physical, psychological, and spiritual *growth*. True growth never stops; it is continual.

Next, challenge your students to come up with examples of how these needs can be met, and how they all can best help each other get their needs met. Discuss ways that these needs can be disturbed, and what can be done to "fix" them. For instance, you could ask this question:

> *If someone is having trouble with one or more of these needs, is it possible that his or her friends and family can help? How?*

When youngsters can handle tough questions like these, they grasp the concept.

I have done this needs lesson with students ages elementary through secondary, and have found their responses sensitive, insightful, and pertinent. I have come back a month or two later, and have found that, as a class, they can come up with all of the seven needs and define them perfectly. Refreshing.

Feelings

We are all emotional creatures. We learn to address our needs through our feelings. There is a direct connection between our ability to feel and the ability to get our needs met. I often describe it this way:

> *If our needs are like bridges that we must cross on our journey through life, feelings are the messengers that tell us when a bridge is out!*

So what happens when we don't get the message? What happens when the computers are down? That's right; disaster. In my work with young people I find it very interesting that many youngsters are "disconnected" from their own feelings (this problem, of course, is not at all unique to children). As a result many youngsters act out their pain and frustration through behaviors that don't always seem to make sense. This sometimes makes it difficult to develop effective intervention and treatment.

Part of the reason we have difficulty in recognizing and utilizing feelings effectively is that we often see the pain of sadness as something to be avoided at all cost. The all-too-typical philosophy is: "If it hurts to hurt, then don't do it." In practice there's only one problem with this thinking: it's wrong. It simply doesn't work that way. Much more damage can be done denying feelings than recognizing them.

Pictured here is a chart of just four feelings. When I teach this model to young people, I call it "The Upside-Down 'T' of

Feelings." The direction of growth is up. The model shows *mad* and *scared* as being "sideways." They are valid and important emotions, but it is important that a person not experience them long enough to grow permanently attached to them. (Have you ever known a person whose feelings had shut down to anger and fear—and they seemed to *like* it that way?)

These four feelings, *sad, mad, glad,* and *scared,* are critical "messengers" for everyone to understand and utilize. To understand them, and to use them effectively, is to move toward healing and recovery. And healing and recovery are necessary for recapturing spontaneity.

I'm often asked: "Why only *four* feelings?" Simple; until we can handle four, it makes no sense to learn more.

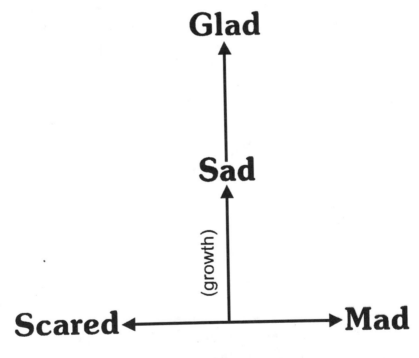

The Feelings Model

When a youngster is in better touch with his or her feelings, it becomes possible to talk through the difficulties, and not act them out with inappropriate behavior. Consequently, not only do youngsters learn a skill for handling life, you as a teacher will have fewer behavioral episodes to handle. Everyone wins; everyone grows.

Show your students the Feelings Model by drawing it on the board. If they seem surprised that there are only four feelings, explain that these are just the basics, the beginning. Assure them, however, that if they can recognize these feelings in themselves and others, and respond appropriately to them, they will gain a tremendous amount of power in their lives. Remind them that happiness is not the *absence* of problems; it's the ability to *handle* the problems.

I enjoy pointing out to youngsters that the feeling of *sad* is in the center of the chart for a reason. *Sad* is the most critical of the four. In fact, the ability to process sadness authentically and effectively when it occurs is actually the safest and most direct avenue back to emotional equilibrium and genuine happiness. Since sadness is about some kind of loss (if nothing else, it is the loss of gladness), even fear and anger must eventually be processed as loss (the loss of *not* being afraid, or the loss of *not* being angry). At that point the individual moves beyond fear and anger.

Share with your students that sadness carries one great benefit: it is one feeling that draws to it the assistance and soothing of others. In other words, sadness brings corporate support, hope, and nurturance. (Whenever there is a death in the family, friends, neighbors, and church members bring you their support *and* a chicken casserole. Call your best friend to tell them that your daughter or niece just earned a scholarship to Stanford, and you'll get a resounding, "Congratulations." But you *won't* get a casserole!) And yet it is precisely the feeling of sadness that many folks want to mask or deny.

With these thoughts in mind, here are some activities that incorporate the feelings of *sad, mad, glad,* and *scared.*

The Needs chart and the Feelings Model appeared in the previously referenced book *If My Kid's So Nice ... Why's He Driving ME Crazy?* by James D. Sutton (Friendly Oaks Publications, 1997). They are reprinted here with permission.

#29

Feelings brainstorm

This is an important activity as other feelings activities come from it. Also, this activity can give you material for practicing the skills of brainstorming (#79 in chapter six). Use this process for the brainstorming.

Starting with one of the four feelings, let your students brainstorm it by coming up with as many situations as possible which demonstrate it. (This proves to be an excellent exercise in that it helps students clarify differences among the four feelings. For instance, it's easy to confuse feelings like fear and anger.) You could even give them an assignment to notice sad things (if that is the feeling of focus) in their community, in the newspaper, in television programs, and in movies.

After you have a healthy collection of examples, type them onto cards. Here are some examples:

SAD:

- **Jay's mother told him that his grandmother had died.**
- **Timmy studied hard for his spelling test, but he failed it.**

MAD:

- The umpire said that Jimmy was out when he tried to steal second base. Jimmy was sure that he was safe.
- Someone took the money from Mary's piggy bank. She was going to use it to go swimming with her friends.

GLAD:

- Mrs. Deaver, Sue's next-door neighbor, promised Sue that she could have one of her dog's puppies.
- Mr. Jones gave Billy a summer job cleaning the parking lot at his grocery store.

SCARED:

- Mark's principal called him into the office and told him that his father had been in an automobile accident.
- Big Luke told Tommy that he was going to beat him up after school.

#30

Feelings role play

Here's an excellent activity for Cooperative Learning groups. Take the activity cards that were created and spread them out on a table face down. Let a student or a group select a card, then role-play the scenario on the card. See how quickly the other youngsters can guess the feeling they are portraying.

Expand this same idea into art activities by letting the youngsters make stick, hand, or finger puppets out of socks, paper bags, sticks and paper plates, construction paper, and similar materials. Then let them act out their feelings activity card for the class. This activity not only helps youngsters understand and utilize feelings, it provides an excellent opportunity for creativity to take root.

#31

What was lost?

Here's an excellent lesson to help youngsters understand that all sadness and depression are about something that is lost. If nothing else, the feeling of *not* being sad or depressed is lost. Using the following story, or one similar to it, let the youngsters brainstorm as many things as they can think of that were lost (again, it is suggested that you use the process for brainstorming that is covered in activity #79). Another way would be to let youngsters brainstorm in their Cooperative Learning groups. Here's the scene:

> **Johnny is nine years old. He is very sad. His folks are getting a divorce. Johnny and his mother will be moving to another city when school is out. They will be living with Johnny's grandparents. Since depression is about loss, see how many things you can think of that Johnny will lose when he moves.**

If the students need a little help with this activity, suggest that there are tangible and intangible things that he might lose (you'll need to explain *tangible,* then let them help you come up with tangible versus intangible things), as well as obvious losses of relationships. Some examples of things Johnny could lose might include:

TANGIBLES:

- His old home
- His room
- His bed
- His desk at school
- His school
- His church

INTANGIBLES:

- Security and order
- Confidence
- The "way it used to be"
- The earlier standard of living

RELATIONSHIPS:

- Old friends
- His teachers
- His school counselor
- His school principal
- His soccer team and coach
- Father as a regular figure in his life
- Church friends

#32

Ink or oil; which are you?

Here's an activity that demonstrates that we can handle obstacles and frustration in stride, or we can allow ourselves to be *totally* affected by any trouble that comes along.

Fill two beakers or two large, clear glasses with water. This represents life. Show the youngsters two small containers, one containing ink, the other containing motor oil. These represent trouble and problems that can come into our lives. Some people handle trouble as if it were ink; others as if it were oil.

Have a student place one large drop of ink into one glass, and ask everyone to observe carefully what happens. The black of the ink colors *all* the water, just as some folks let a little trouble or difficulty affect everything about them.

Repeat the process by having another student put a drop of motor oil into the other glass. Observation: The oil stays together in a small clump. The rest of the water in the glass is not affected by it. Indeed, there are people who don't let a little trouble totally affect everything about them. They can handle it, and move on.

Finally, take some time to discuss what this activity means, and what can be learned from it.

This idea was contributed anonymously when I presented a program for Louisiana State University.

#33

"Sock It to Me!" scramble

This feelings activity might involve a bit of expense (or some creative begging), but it is well worth it. Secure a large number of plain white crew socks and three bright colors of fabric dye.

Assign a color for each feeling (white plus three others) and dye the socks accordingly. Although it is a bit messy, you might let your Cooperative Learning groups take turns dyeing a bundle of socks.

For the activity, have all of the youngsters remove their shoes. Then place a large box full of the loose socks in the middle of the room (actually "toss" the socks as you would a salad). Let the youngsters draw an activity card (from activity #29), then line up against the wall. At the shout of "Sock It to Me!" let the students race to the box, dive into the socks, and select two appropriately colored socks, put them on, then go back to their desks, a circle, or a carpeted area on the floor. Ask them to discuss their card, which is represented by the socks they are wearing. Then put the socks back into the box, draw cards again, and repeat the activity.

#34

Signs and bumper stickers

Let your students design signs that say something about feelings. Offer prizes for the most creative posters, and display them in the classroom. Here are some examples:

Suffering Permitted Here
30 Minutes Free Parking

American Express Accepted Here
You're American, so go ahead—Express

Tomorrow, at exactly 10:27 a.m.,
I will do something spontaneous.

As a spin-off of this idea, do something similar, but with "one-liner" bumper stickers. If you make these from the right materials, perhaps you could really put them on bumpers. For kids, maybe we need backpack stickers. Now that's an idea. Again, here are some ideas:

I brake for feelings!

Need a smile? Borrow mine!

#35

This spud's for you!

Give each youngster a potato, and have them count off one through four. The number they call corresponds to a feeling (for instance, #3 would be *glad*). They are asked to study their potato carefully, noting every feature of that potato that makes it different from every other potato in the world. They are to give their potato an identity, including sex, name, and age. They are then asked to develop a story about their potato person, using the feeling assigned to them. Each child then talks about his or her potato, telling the story. When the story is finished, each potato goes back into the box.

At the end of all the stories, when the potatoes are all back in the box, the students are asked to find their potato as quickly as possible. Ask them to explain how they were able to pick their potato from all the others in the box (this is an excellent activity for helping youngsters understand that everyone has qualities about them that make them unique).

Another exercise is exactly like "This spud's for you!" only lemons are used instead of potatoes. This makes the whole activity considerably more difficult, requiring keener skills of perception.

Look 'em over carefully, Miss. They ALL look the same to me.

#36

Talk show

Select a student to be the classroom radio station's announcer, complete with a table, a microphone, and a chair for the guest. Give the program a name, and give the station some interesting call letters. The announcer goes "on the air" and introduces a guest. The guest talks about a major problem that he or she is currently experiencing. The announcer invites listeners to call in to offer advice to the guest. A part of the room is set up to look like a telephone booth or a listener's home. Students take turns calling in to help the guest.

Of course you could also work this the other way, with students calling in to talk with the guest "expert" about their problem or concern. This activity provides lots of opportunity for reflection and discussion.

#37

Pot luck

Share with your students that you are going to show them a way that they can use their birthdate and their birth month to create a feelings "word painting." From List A each youngster is to select a feeling that corresponds to their birth month. From the stimulus words in List B, they are to select the words that correspond to the day they were born. Then, on a sheet of paper, they create a story that combines the word and the feeling.

SAD (January)	GLAD (July)
MAD (February)	SCARED (August)
GLAD (March)	SAD (September)
SCARED (April)	MAD (October)
SAD (May)	GLAD (November)
MAD (June)	SCARED (December)

List A

1. flag
2. cowboy boots
3. baseball
4. tricycle
5. puppy
6. calendar
7. car keys
8. sports car
9. chick
10. earring
11. alarm clock
12. balloon
13. Thanskgiving turkey
14. ice cream cone
15. roller skates
16. sunflower
17. Christmas lights
18. kitten
19. necktie
20. checkbook
21. fish
22. Sunday
23. school books
24. TV dinner
25. uniform
26. lawnmower
27. ballpoint pen
28. truck
29. birdhouse
30. tree
31. watch

List B

Here's a sample story that would fit a person who was born on the 16th of June (Mad Sunflower):

You know, sometimes it seems like even a sunflower can't get a decent break. You see, I love the sun. I love to admire it all day long. But there's

67

this bunch of bees that keep walking on my face and stepping in my eyes. It's like they have no consideration for a hard-working plant. I get so mad sometimes that I feel like going over to their hive and dropping a few petals in their way. Maybe then they'd get the message that what they do really upsets me.

This one, Glad Baseball (for November 3, for example), was printed in the December 1990 edition of our newsletter *Reaching Out*:

This box is so dark. I wish I could go out and fly through the air. I think I hear someone coming into the equipment room. Oh, it is! Maybe today will be my day for the big one. The thought of the big game thrills me. Oh joy, someone is getting my box and carrying me off.

The man in black is opening the box and taking me out. The lights are bright and there are shouts of joy everywhere. The man in black carefully walks across the field with me safely nestled in his little black bag. He reaches in, cradles me in his hand, lifts me out, and gently places me in the hands of a master.

With great skill the master begins to hurl me through the air to my targeted mitt across the field. I am ecstatic. My ecstasy increases as the night goes on, and the cheers increase as my master nears his goal. Finally the last out comes and I realize that I have played a part in making history as the baseball behind Nolan Ryan's 300th win!

Pretty good, huh? This last one, Scared Flag (it could work for August 1), was in the same newsletter. Remember Desert Storm?

> **I used to be confident and courageous. I flew high—red, white, and blue. I knew that I stood for America, freedom, and democracy. I was respected, saluted, and cared for. Somehow that's changed, and I'm scared. Instead of feeling confident, I'm taken for granted and I wonder what's going to happen to me.**
>
> **I find myself sewn to the bottom of blue jeans. I'm spat upon all over the world. Friends of mine have even been burned. It used to be safe to be a flag, but now it's risky. Today I was called to go to Saudi Arabia, where anything is possible.**
>
> **I can hardly sleep at night wondering and worrying about my fate. The desert will dry out my threads, fade my colors, and cover me in sand. I may be shot full of holes and never return home. My ancestors faced similar risks in previous wars, so I'm expected to do my part.**
>
> **But frankly, I'm scared.**

Glad Baseball was written by Janis Moore of LaVernia, Texas. Credit for Scared Flag goes to Jessica Star, a school counselor for Cambridge Elementary School in San Antonio, Texas.

#38

Is the disk ever full?

Here's an idea that was initially shared to demonstrate the nature of knowledge, but it also can remind us of the value of others.

Show your students a blank 3.5-inch floppy disk (although you could also use a compact disk). Engage them in this discussion:

Class, what am I holding?

(A computer disk.)

If this disk is blank, what is it worth?

(It's worth only a few cents.)

It's almost worthless, isn't it?

For effect, toss the disk onto the floor, and "accidentally" step on it as you walk across the room.

By the way, a blank disk like this weighs only .7 of an ounce. Not much at all. That's about what three sheets of paper and an envelope weigh.

But what if I were to store something really valuable on this disk, like the cure for all cancer. What would it be worth then?

(A lot; a whole lot!)

I'd take better care of it, wouldn't I? I would treat it differently.

Pick the disk up, dust it off, and gently place it on the desk.

And, when it is a full disk, containing a cure for cancer, what does it weigh then? Actually it weighs exactly the same as it weighed when it was empty, because, in the manner that the disk stores information, knowledge doesn't weigh anything.

At this point you might want to ask your students to think of how many ways information can be stored on something as simple as a floppy disk. Here is some input that came from students:

- **Words (text, as in the cure for cancer)**
- **Pictures**
- **Motion video**
- **Sounds**
- **Numbers (bank accounts and credit cards)**
- **Games**

How are people like this floppy disk?

(They can also become more valuable as they learn.)

Can we help others to fill their disks?

(Yes.)

Is it possible sometimes that mean folks can try to erase some or all of the disks of others?

(Yes.)

How might they try to do this?

(By telling someone that they are stupid, or that they are not important. Sometimes there is even abuse. That could erase parts of a person's disk.)

Would a person who has part or all of their disk erased have trouble? How?

(Yes, they might not be very confident, and they might be so nervous and afraid that they couldn't learn very well. They might be scared that someone was going to erase their disk some more.)

How could we help them?

Youngsters can provide a lot of answers to this last question, but basically this kind of help would cause a person to feel safe and let them know that we are there to help them fill their disk again.

The idea for this activity came from Glenna Salsbury of Paradise Valley, California. Glenna is a fellow speaker and past president of the National Speakers Association, and a top-shelf human being.

The last six ideas and activities in this section encourage youngsters to go beyond learning for learning's sake to apply skills of understanding and caring to others, and, of course, to themselves.

#39

The Sunshine Post Office

A few years back I was a consulting psychologist for a residential treatment facility for young people. Our most challenging unit housed adolescent girls. We hit upon an idea of small individual mailboxes. These mailboxes were all connected, much like the ones you see in the post office. Each girl, using markers and paint, individualized the door to her own mailbox (they were *definitely* unique).

This idea was a hit. Girls not only received their regular mail in their mailbox, they were able to send and receive mail from the staff and from each other. It was stressed that they encourage each other with their letters and notes, and it was a rule that every note had to be signed.

I soon discovered that some girls could better express themselves in writing, plus, of course, they had time to compose what they wanted to say. Many of them saved every piece of this "affirmation mail," re-reading it often. It was a powerful idea.

The same concept can easily be done at school. The mailboxes can be plain or fancy. It might even work to section off a large bulletin board into individual squares that youngsters can decorate. Mail could be tacked in place with push-pins.

For the teacher, this is little more than another form of "Wonging," but it is unique in that it provides a process for youngsters to "Wong" each other. Suggestion: Encourage youngsters to watch the mailboxes and to make an effort to affirm someone who hasn't received some mail in a while.

I was the consulting psychologist for Buckner Treatment Center in San Antonio, Texas, from October of 1986 to October of 1996. During those ten years I worked with the best staff on this planet, and I saw deep and positive changes in many of the young lives that lived there.

#40

Hearts apart

Here's an excellent activity for teaching empathy and sensitivity. Give each youngster a large heart cut from a piece of construction paper, or let them do this themselves. Have them write their name on their heart. Then ask them to exchange hearts with another person.

Tell your students that you are going to read five of the *sad* cards that were created in Activity #29. After you read a card, ask each youngster to tear off a piece of the heart they are holding. The piece they tear off should correspond to how they think the heart's owner would be affected by what has been read. Remind them not to respond as they themselves would, but as the heart's owner would respond. Have them number the pieces, with the first card being #1, the second being #2, and so on. After doing this through all five cards, each student should have a heart in six pieces.

Give the students a one-page handout of the content of the five cards, and let them share and reflect how they handled each one as they considered their classmate's heart. Let them tape the hearts back together, write a supportive comment on the back, and give them back to their owners.

Be certain to allow some time for the youngsters to completely process this valuable activity.

Thanks to Stephanie Waters, a school counselor from Laplace, Louisiana, for this great idea.

#41

I remember Grandma

Here's an interesting activity that stresses heritage and the affirmation of loved ones from the past. It connects youngsters to their roots, and helps them understand that the things that make folks last in memory are those things that touch others.

Ask your students to talk to their parents about someone

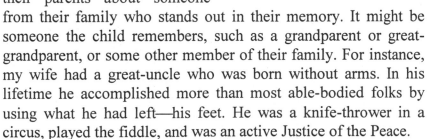

from their family who stands out in their memory. It might be someone the child remembers, such as a grandparent or great-grandparent, or some other member of their family. For instance, my wife had a great-uncle who was born without arms. In his lifetime he accomplished more than most able-bodied folks by using what he had left—his feet. He was a knife-thrower in a circus, played the fiddle, and was an active Justice of the Peace.

Have your students prepare a ten-minute presentation about their "I Remember" person. Then, as they conclude, they place a carnation in a vase. When the arrangement is complete, take the flowers to a nursing home (this ties in to activity # 89).

What follows is part of the story I told when I did this activity with a group of girls at Buckner Treament Center in San Antonio, Texas. I honored my mother's mother, Myrtle Harriet Smith—my grandmother.

For a number of years I was the only grandchild on my mother's side of the family. For that reason, my grandmother and I had a very special relationship.

One of my favorite memories about her goes back to a time when I spent most of the summer with her and my aunt's family in Minnesota. I was about nine at the time.

Grandma and I made the return trip to Tulsa, Oklahoma, by train. Those were the days when only the well-to-do could even dream of traveling by air.

Armed with a couple of sacks of books, games, and snack foods, Grandma and I boarded the train and settled into our seats for the two-day trip. I can still remember watching the scenery go by on my first train ride, drifting in and out of sleep to the clickity-clack of steel on steel.

For those folks riding through the night in coach (instead of the expensive Pullman cars), the porter would make his way down the aisle renting pillows. We only needed one. Grandma, an experienced traveler by rail, always carried her own fine down pillow with her.

Morning found us making a rest stop. Grandma treated me to a hearty breakfast in the station cafeteria; then we boarded again. When we returned to our seats, we noticed that the porter

had taken up all of the pillows—including Grandma's! She insisted that the porter sort through the piles of pillows until he retrieved the one that belonged to her.

I suppose that traveling by train with Grandma stands out in my mind because it was a very special adventure that we shared. Through the years we did a lot of things together. She even taught me how to embroider a little, and how to bake sugar cookies.

I was home on leave from the Navy in 1968 when she passed away. I was just a couple of days from leaving for a two-year hitch in Japan. She was very sick, but she *knew* that I was still home. To this day, I think she picked her time.

I've heard that these things happen.

"I Remember Grandma" is reprinted with permission from the book *Windows* by James D. Sutton (Friendly Oaks Publications, 1991).

#42

The Victory List

Some youngsters can be so down on themselves that they fail to recognize their own accomplishments and improvement. Here's an idea that can be incorporated into a written language activity. It stresses self-affirmation.

Try this activity on a Friday afternoon. Give each student a copy of the Victory List and ask them to list their three most significant "victories" for the week. Remind them that they don't have to be big victories, just *their* victories.

Give the class an opportunity to share what they listed, what it means to them, and whether they have made any additional plans or goals for the next week.

If you have a small class, or have youngsters work in Cooperative Learning groups, you could even have the students also fill out Victory Lists on each other, then compare.

The Victory List is from *If My Kid's So Nice ... Why's He Driving ME Crazy?* by James D. Sutton (Friendly Oaks Publications, 1997). It is reprinted here with permission.

My Victory List

1. _____

_____

2. _____

_____

3. _____

_____

#43

The patch

I found out about this great idea from a student who visited my office. He was wearing a large school patch; it was attached to one leg of his jeans, dangling from a safety pin. Obviously, I asked a few questions, and followed up with a call to his teacher.

The teacher starts out the school year by awarding the patch to one student who has demonstrated good behavior and is especially thoughtful and helpful to others. This student gets to wear the patch for the week, and is instructed to look for the most deserving student to wear the patch the following week. All of this is charted, with the intent to pass the patch around to as many youngsters as possible throughout the school year.

Exactly what is the patch? The teacher said she cut it off the sleeve of an old high school band uniform. The patch and the idea behind it mean a lot to her and her class.

Since visiting with the child who first showed me the patch, I have had the opportunity to work with other students from the same class. They have all expressed what a privilege it is to wear the patch, and how they aspire to wear it again.

This idea was shared by Norma Proffitt, fourth-grade teacher at Pettus Elementary School, Pettus, Texas.

#44

John Glenn's locker

Everyone knows John Glenn, the ex-astronaut who returned into space aboard the space shuttle *Discovery* in October of 1998 at the age of 77. Apparently, in his hometown of New Concord, Ohio, John has continued to be a hero after his historic Mercury flight of 1962. Locker #145 at New Concord Elementary School was Glenn's when he was a student there. And all the students know it. Today, John Glenn's old school locker is reserved for the second-grader demonstrating the best performance and behavior. They have a hero's locker for a week.

Now you might not have John Glenn's locker at your school, but think about how you might be able to set aside a locker or a special chair in the lunchroom (complete with head-of-the-line privileges) for a youngster who has demonstrated the most helping attitude toward others.

This idea was inspired by an article that appeared in the October 30, 1998, edition of *USA Today* (section 3A).

Chapter Five

Accomplishing Classwork with a Flair

Breaking the "ho-hum" barrier

Task completion at school is important. No, that's not exactly true; it is *critical*. And, with more and more expectations being placed upon youngsters to produce academically, compliance has become a serious issue at school. Too many youngsters have learned how to beat the whole system by simply shutting down.

I call it "victory by default." It's not what the youngster is doing that is so problematic; it's what he is *not* doing. And we're talking about youngsters who are otherwise pretty good kids. Their substantial numbers are causing a meltdown in some schools today. Why? Because school operates on a foundation of compliance.

Think about it; if all the students in your school start to evacuate the building at exactly 10:00 a.m., what are the teachers and administrators going to do to stop them?

Nothing, that's what. Oh, a really quick teacher might be able to tackle one or two as they zip by, but that's about it. The whole system is built upon compliance, so when three or four students in a classroom begin to go on strike, it doesn't take long for problems to compound—quickly.

This behavior is so prevalent with youngsters within the schools today that we have a name for it: *oppositional and defiant.* In its more severe form the condition is diagnosed as oppositional defiant disorder. Today, ODD is running a close second to ADHD (attention deficit hyperactivity disorder) as a primary behavioral condition of children and adolescents. In fact, it's not uncommon for youngsters to be diagnosed with *both* disorders (psychologists call this *comorbidity*). Since school is the foremost compliance environment (Johnny isn't going to fail family if he doesn't make his bed, but he *can* fail the fourth grade), teachers are very aware of ADHD and ODD at school.

"WE WERE RIGHT COMMANDER. THERE'S NO VISIBLE SIGN OF ANY LIFE DOWN HERE."

Even if a youngster is not so defiant, that child can become frustrated and bored when everything at school fails to break the "ho-hum" barrier. And this applies to teachers too. Of what use are school and district-wide academic goals and objectives if they don't contain something that motivates students (and teachers) to accomplish them? In other words, where's the "buy-in"?

This chapter contains 32 ideas and activities for achieving more compliance. Granted, they will not permanently alter the face of education, but they might make task completion a bit more consistent—and, hopefully, considerably more fun.

Five guidelines for task compliance

The task compliance ideas and activities covered in this section will follow one or several of the following five guidelines:

Guideline #1: Add to; don't take away

A teacher in Kansas shared that this was the main idea she took away from my workshop, and it made a dramatic difference in her classroom.

Frankly, some folks bristle at the notion of "adding to." It's not difficult picking this teacher out in a crowd. He's the one teaching at the end of his rope and at the top of his lungs. And all the while he's complaining that his students are doing less than nothing. Consider that basing a system on penalties ("taking away") can throw the door wide open to arguing, blaming, excuse-making, and the rapid deterioration of relationships. Besides, it's a fact that negative consequences for noncompliance are having less and less effect in today's classroom (probably because the teacher's frustration is a much bigger pay-off than any benefits for compliance).

Hmm; does this mean that the behaviors of some youngsters are more influenced by our anger than our teaching skills? Of course. It happens all the time.

"Adding to" represents a change in direction. In concept, "adding to" makes it interesting and appealing for a youngster to comply. Since there is no pay-off for noncompliance, compliance becomes a clearer alternative.

But the simple truth is that we cannot ignore noncompliance indefinitely, especially within a learning environment. But if we can ignore it long enough to convert the system to "added to," it is possible to accomplish more—sometimes a whole lot more.

Activities such as "The Great Banana Split Race" (#47) and "Extra Point Pop Quiz" (#54) are excellent examples of "adding to."

Pat Zimmerman is the teacher from Kansas. She teaches fifth grade in Grantville.

Guideline #2: Minimize verbal redirection

We talk too much. If that's not clear enough, here it is again: we *talk* too much! When we talk too much, most of our words fall to the floor and get swept away. Our lips are moving, but they just don't hear us anymore.

Suggestion: Emphasize nonverbal redirection. It helps. As a bonus, nonverbal redirection reduces excuses and the backlash that might erupt from a frustrated or easily embarrassed student (yes, *both* of these conditions are on the increase). In my training programs I often ask this question:

What do you really want from the child who is off task? Do you want redirection, or a pound of flesh?

A lot of teachers will *say* that they want redirection, but then they go for the pound of flesh. Results: They can eventually get that pound all right, but only if they're willing to give up two or three of their own.

"The 'Good Medicine' Plan" (#69) and "Time tab" (#71) are examples of activities that emphasize nonverbal redirection.

Guideline #3: Provide relief points

One way to ensure a miserable time for you and your class is to put students on a long, sustained, difficult task. Trouble is not a matter of *if,* but *when.* It's much like sending kids off on a barefoot trip across an ocean of burning coals. Few of them will survive either the trip or the coals. Provide relief points.

If we don't build in a few compliance breaks, kids will find creative ways to take them anyway. What's needed is a coffee break—only without the coffee. By sanctioning an occasional "coffee break" in a lesson, compliance can be reinforced, and youngsters will focus more closely on the task if they know the break is coming. "The pencil nap" (#68) is an activity which provides relief points.

A final note about this guideline: Although providing relief points is beneficial to a classroom spirit of compliance, two things are important to keep in mind. First, breaks should be at random, and not become too predictable (in some instances too much predictability can work against you). Second, helping youngsters to build upon their skills of tolerance and improve their abilities to work more productively on long and difficult tasks is *also* of great importance. Gradually putting more time between the relief points is one way to increase tolerance and compliance.

Guideline #4: Enable self-evaluation

Providing youngsters opportunity to evaluate themselves is not only empowering, it encourages personal responsibility. Surprisingly enough, when students are allowed to self-evaluate, they are often tougher on themselves than a teacher would be.

Self-evaluation of behavior and achievement in daily assignments and activities is an excellent way to begin. The activity "Self-evaluate" (#76) demonstrates this guideline.

Guideline #5: Give humor a little space

The value of spontaneity has already been discussed as a quality found in youngsters who are comfortable and confident with themselves. Humor develops naturally within an environment that acknowledges and encourages spontaneity. Laughter is both healthy and constructive, and it should be encouraged.

"Jumper cables" (#67) is an idea that encourages and elicits the best qualities of humor.

#45

School attendance; it's in the cards

All the best strategies for directing students to tasks aren't going to be worth a rip if they won't come to school. Here's a creative idea that was shared with me in person by Mario, an elementary school principal.

Mario first came upon the idea of using sports trading cards with students when his son went off to college. The boy left behind quite a collection of cards, so Mario took them to school. He started using them before school on bad weather days.

Mario would approach youngsters and ask them, "What's four times eight?" Whenever he got a correct answer, he would give a trading card as a prize. When a youngster offered to trade cards with him, Mario hit upon a way to boost school attendance. For a student to trade cards with him, that student would have to bring their card to school the next day. Before long, Mario was trading for anything that even *looked* like a trading card. It didn't matter, because the cards kept the kids coming to school. Overall school attendance increased significantly.

Eventually Mario began to offer trading cards as prizes for perfect attendance every six weeks. It was a good news, bad news situation. The good news: Attendance figures climbed. The bad news: Mario was running out of trading cards. He bought some from suppliers, but it was too expensive.

He decided to ask for autographed cards from the athletes themselves. All Pro tight end Jay Novacek of the Dallas Cowboys (now retired) was the first to answer the call. He sent six autographed cards, one for each six weeks of the school year. Autographed cards came in from John Elway, Troy Aikman, Derrick Thomas, Darrell Green, and others. Chicago Bear Chris Zorich sent cards, photographs, and even a glove he had worn in a game.

And that was just football. Mario had an excellent response from athletes in other sports as well.

Today, if you stroll through the library of Mario's school, you will find a huge display case full of autographed trading cards, tee-shirts, photos, and all sorts of attendance awards that have been donated by professional athletes. You might have a little trouble taking a look into the case because of all the youngsters who are making plans about the items they are going to earn.

At last contact, Mario's school was running 98% attendance. And this is in a part of the country where school attendance has typically been a problem.

Mario Hernandez is the principal of North Bridge Elementary School in Weslaco, Texas.

#46

Establish the P.A.C.E.

P.A.C.E. stands for *participation, attitude, cooperation,* and *effort.* For any given grade-reporting period (some schools use six weeks, others nine weeks), a full 25% of a youngster's grade in a subject is based on how well the child has participated in class (such as raising a hand when questions are asked), whether their attitude was positive, how well they cooperated with the teacher and with classmates, and how much effort they put into doing their work. The remaining 75% of every student's grade for the reporting period consists of exams (25%), projects (25%), and homework (25%).

P.A.C.E. grades are an excellent way of leveling the playing field a bit for youngsters who are less capable in terms of innate ability and skill. These students can compensate through good prosocial habits and old-fashioned hustle.

P.A.C.E. scores are kept weekly. A maximum of 20 P.A.C.E. points are achievable each day according to the teacher's evaluation of the youngster's *participation, attitude, cooperation,* and *effort.* This creates a potential P.A.C.E. score of 100% for the week. The weekly scores are then averaged for a P.A.C.E. grade at the end of the reporting period.

Note that youngsters have the opportunity to add as many as 20 points to their P.A.C.E. grade daily. This follows the guideline of "adding to," as opposed to starting off with 100% P.A.C.E. points each week, then deducting points for inappropriate behavior. Although both ways will get you the same score at the end of the week, "adding to" focuses on positives rather than negatives.

The P.A.C.E. grade was shared by Brenda Gearhart of Williamsport, Pennsylvania. She teaches social studies at Williamsport High School, and is also a Licensed Social Worker.

#47

The Great Banana Split Race

Although this idea was initially used to promote good behavior and citizenship, it could also be used to encourage students to complete assignments and turn them in promptly.

Here's how it works: Each week of the reporting period provides an opportunity for a youngster to earn a component of a banana split. Then, at the end of the reporting period, youngsters receive the parts of the dessert they have earned. The parts accumulate as follows (using an example of a nine-week reporting period):

Week #1: a spoon
Week #2: a dish
Week #3: a sliced banana
Week #4: a scoop of chocolate ice cream
Week #5: a scoop of vanilla ice cream
Week #6: a scoop of strawberry ice cream
Week #7: toppings
Week #8: whipped cream
Week #9: chopped nuts

A cherry for the top is thrown in as a bonus for a perfect nine weeks. All of this is charted each week so that everyone's progress is easily tracked.

All components of the banana split must be earned in order. This means that a child who does not earn a spoon at the end of the first week must work for the spoon during the second week (while others are going for the dish). Here is the "adding to" principle working to the max. The wake-up call for some youngsters comes on banana split day. If they have earned only a spoon, that's all they get—a spoon. Rarely does a child get caught with only a spoon at the end of the next Great Banana Split Race. Four races can be held during the school year (or six, if you have a six-week reporting period).

This idea was shared by Teresa Chambers. She teaches at Sharpe Accelerated Elementary School in Memphis, Tennessee.

#48

Homework helper

Here's an idea for encouraging a specific youngster to complete a homework assignment. Ask the student to be your Homework Helper, assigning them the "honor" of helping the class check the homework assignment the next day.

The position of Homework Helper is promoted as a special privilege. The idea is that this youngster is likely to be better prepared the next day, knowing they will be in front of the class.

At the junior high or high school level, the position could be called the "ATA"—Assigned Teaching Assistant.

Thanks to LeEster Burch for this idea. She teaches second grade in Pflugerville, Texas.

#49

Build your own exam

Back in the "old days" students who did well in homework and unit tests were exempt from the final exam. This was quite an incentive for a youngster to do well on daily and weekly work. This idea spins off from this concept.

Alert your students about the structure and scope of the upcoming unit test (true/false, essay, multiple choice, short answer, fill-in-the-blank, and matching, as well as the number of items on the exam). As students complete and turn in daily assignments, projects, and weekly tests, they can "build" their unit exam by earning fewer test items, or developing more of the type of test items they'd prefer. Of course they never see the actual test until they take it, but through their compliance they know exactly how the test will be structured, and how many items will be on it. The only thing you have given them is the opportunity to do their work without complaint and improve their overall grade in the process. Not a bad bargain.

It is also possible for students to structure the difficulty level of the exam, as in the game show Jeopardy. Use your creativity here; these ideas empower as they stress, without pressure, the values of compliance and planning.

Brenda Gearhart, the teacher who shared the P.A.C.E. grade idea, brainstormed this idea with me at a workshop at Penn State.

#50

Handmade paper

Youngsters might be more excited about a written assignment if they made the paper they wrote it on. You might want to check some references on this, but I have been led to believe that making paper is not that difficult. It's pretty messy, but not difficult.

Basically, here's how you do it. Have the youngsters collect clean paper products of all types, then cut or tear them up into very small bits (this should hold their attention for a little while). Put these into a large bowl, and pour in warm water and perhaps a little white glue to bind it. Have the youngsters knead this mixture until it has a thick and consistent texture. Add coloring, then place the paper pulp on a screen and press the water out of it. If you intend to do much of this, a simple press can be made out of wood which would facilitate the process. Let it dry completely, and there you have it. Some folks put spices, herbs, and perfumes into the paper also. It's quite impressive.

I know one woman who worked with severely behaviorally disordered youngsters. The kids enjoyed making paper in this way, and they were creative. One youngster began a successful "business" of making note cards and envelopes. Because they are unique, they draw a good price.

Paper made in this manner is precious and scarce, so encourage youngsters to write rough drafts before they transfer their work to the homemade paper.

Handmade paper is also an art form. It can be framed (especially in shadow box frames) and appropriately lit to make a stunning wall accessory. Lots of ideas here, huh?

#51

Pen or pencil swap

Have each youngster decorate a pen or pencil (specify one or the other) in a way that is uniquely "them." Put all of these pens or pencils in a shoebox and have the youngsters draw their writing implement. At the end of that assignment, "shuffle" the pens and do it again when tasks change.

#52

Slip and draw

Every time a student turns in an assignment, give them a slip of paper to sign and drop into a box. At the end of the week, have a drawing for a prize. Youngsters catch on quickly that the more slips they have in the box, the better their chances at winning.

Many educators are trying to cut back on giving students rewards for doing what they should be doing anyway. This strategy only offers a child a *chance* at a reward, making it an excellent transition approach for cutting back on tangible rewards.

#53

Garbage pull

This could be a spin-off of the "Slip and draw," or a unique approach all its own. A Special Education teacher in Texas shared this one. She would put candy and trinkets into a small plastic garbage can. Whenever a youngster did an exceptional job, or finished a difficult assignment, she would offer them a "garbage pull." The child would cover  his eyes and draw from the can. Students loved it, and worked hard for a "pull." There were always a couple of these cans in the room, with a larger one on her desk. This way, she could offer the child a "pull" at her desk or at the student's seat.

Wanda Popp teaches Special Education at Dawson Elementary School in Wharton, Texas. She has been using the "Garbage pull" effectively for many years.

#54

Extra point pop quiz

"Add to; don't take away" (the second guideline) is a good phrase to keep in mind when working with students. If you attempt to take away points, grades, or whatever, you will run the risk of an episode with a youngster. On the other hand, adding to can encourage youngsters to engage in tasks.

Here's one way to do it. Prepare an "extra point" quiz, something that any student could pass if they are reasonably aware of the material covered. In other words, the test would be easy for any youngster who has been awake in class or has looked over the assignment.

Stand at the door and pass out the extra point quizzes to the students as they come through the door. This can even be incorporated with the "Wonging" affirmations.

Put away the extra point quiz as the tardy bell rings. Sure, a few students might trickle in late. When you ask for the quizzes, one of the late ones is bound to say, "Hey, I didn't get one of those." Simply respond with something like:

That's strange. I stood there at the door and handed an extra point pop quiz to every single person who walked into the classroom. I only put them away when the tardy bell rang.

Let students know that they can exchange five of these correct quizzes for their lowest daily grade. This approach not only offers more incentive for achievement, it suggests that you will continue this particular strategy (although it would make sense *not* to do it every day).

If any youngster persists that he or she had a reason for being late and should be able to take the extra point quiz, you have only to point out that the quiz is *extra* point; there is no penalty for not taking it.

This strategy makes it attractive for a youngster to comply. Teachers who have used this technique share that it quickly solves most of the problem of tardies. It also offers a way for youngsters to bring up low daily grades.

This idea was shared by a teacher during a program at the University of Missouri. I did not get a name.

#55

Homework pass

Here's an idea that is simple, easy to implement, and effective. Whenever a student turns in a daily assignment and makes a grade of 90 or better on it, they are given one homework pass. Five such passes can drop the student's lowest daily grade.

This homework pass idea came from Sally Taylor, teacher at Morgantown Elementary in Natchez, Mississippi.

#56

Mint to be

This one is similar to #54, but without the quiz. It recognizes timely compliance.

Place candy, pencils, or other small gifts that the youngsters would enjoy in a bowl near the door to the classroom. As the youngsters come into the classroom, ask them to take their pick, or simply place a sign by them. For instance, if you provided some mint candies, you could provide a sign that says "You're Worth a Mint!" When the tardy bell rings, simply remove the bowl.

Although it is possible to have these "goodies" already on the students' desks when they come into the classroom, with the plan of collecting the items from those desks that are not occupied when the bell rings, there is the possibility of a hassle from a student who walks into the classroom only to see you removing what you have given. This gets into "take away," and it might create problems. Having the "goodies" at the door solves this problem.

Another approach would be to provide the same goodies for youngsters as they complete their work. It is more conditional, but certainly appropriate and effective.

Tom Smart, a teacher from Gresham, Oregon, inspired these ideas.

#57

Best effort bonus

Here's still a different twist on the issue of compliance, an application of the "Add to" guideline.

Make up a test, but add a bonus question. Make it a fairly easy question, the correct answer to which will substantially boost the grade. It is a condition, however, that all other test items *must* be answered before any student can opt for the bonus question. Goal: Nothing will be left blank. All youngsters are encouraged to give every question their best effort.

This idea was shared by a high school coach at a program at the University of Hartford. Sorry, I don't have a name.

#58

The big apple

One principal takes a large ceramic apple full of candy with him into the classroom. He asks teachers how the students are doing. If they are doing well, he gives them all a piece of candy from the apple.

Some youngsters might think that the candy idea is a bit beneath them. They might be more interested in a sticker or a homework pass.

Steve Coston is the principal with the apple. He is responsible for grades kindergarten through twelve at Mullin ISD, Mullin, Texas.

#59

Choices

Lest this strategy be misunderstood, it is important to emphasize that not everything is open to choice. One advantage to offering youngsters choices is that it should support those instances when choice is not an option. Sometimes there is nothing else to do except the task at hand. This is important because youngsters need to know that some things are clearly not negotiable. This is how the "real world" works. But youngsters also need to know how to handle those situations and circumstances that *are* negotiable.

Making choice available can bring balance, increased compliance, and less hassle and misery. (Those few folks who actually *prefer* hassles and misery probably wouldn't care much about compliance anyway.) Kids are more apt to act upon what they have selected.

Establish your criteria for a week's worth of work for a student (although this could just as easily be done with a whole class). Let's say three assignments; they can be turned in as they are completed, but all three are due no later than the end of class (or that subject) Friday. Give the youngsters *more* than you want them to complete (approximately five to ten). Explain that any assignments not selected can be discarded or returned. This can look like an exceptional deal to the youngster if you include some extremely difficult work in the stack. A kid would have to be brain-dead to select it, but it does make the other choices look attractive. Make it easy on yourself; you don't have to spend a lot of time making multiple worksheets or assignments. You can easily cut and paste parts of the same worksheets to give them a different look. Order can be switched, illustrations can be changed or rearranged, and even the types of problems (true-false, multiple choice, matching, short answer, or essay) can be shuffled.

To encourage compliance, make one of the assignments so short and easy it can be completed in 10 minutes or less. Then make certain that the youngster has at least 20 minutes to work on it. This is to create a sense of momentum. The youngster is able to complete the first assignment on Monday, and can even begin the second one during the remainder of Monday's work period. Of course the second and third assignments are much longer and more involved, but this perception of progress early in the week can be encouraging.

Occasionally there will be that student who is oppositional and defiant *regardless* of the choices you provide. If so, try something else (that's why this book is called *101 Ways*).

#60
Living color choices

Try this one when you are offering choices to a whole class. Time might not permit you to make up a wide selection of worksheets, but you could offer the assignments in a variety of colors. This idea not only empowers through choice, the *color* of the paper can actually make a difference.

Another option would be to offer a limited number of worksheets, but place a different sticker on each worksheet (be certain to select stickers that students would like). They can choose the assignment *and* the sticker.

#61
Timers

Once when I was working in the public schools I went over to a Special Education classroom to help a teacher prepare for an IEP (Individualized Education Plan) meeting. Onc student was way off task.

"Mark, if you don't get busy, I'm going to put you on a timer," she noted.

The kid paled. "Oh no, Miss, not the timer. Please, not the timer!" He got back to work.

I was amazed. "Jan, what is it about the timer?"

"I have no idea," she replied. "I just know that it works."

As best I can figure, timers have a very positive effect in redirecting many youngsters back to task, and it seems to work pretty well with all age groups.

The reason timers are so effective might be up for grabs, but I think that the competitive spirit in kids is engaged whenever a teacher plops a timer down with a challenge of, "See if you can finish that worksheet before the timer goes off."

Of course, this strategy will quickly lose its appeal if it is used too much. For maximum benefit, use timers sparingly.

Janis Moore was the teacher. She is now an Educational Diagnostician for LaVernia Schools in LaVernia, Texas. Jan also wrote Glad Baseball in activity #37.

#62
Music box

To apply a similar strategy with a different look, use a small music box. Obviously this would work best when a youngster has only a small amount of work to complete. Wind up the music box, set it down next to the assignment, and challenge the youngster to finish before the music stops.

#63
Spit in the soup

While having lunch with a friend, you suddenly lean over and spit in their soup. Now there are a lot of things you could say to explain such a gesture, but you couldn't say, "Oh, excuse me; *that* was an accident!" Spitting in your friend's soup would be a Class A provocative gesture. There would be no other way to explain it.

And it *will* bring a response.

Unexpected provocative gestures can be used in the classroom precisely because they bring on a response. In other instances a provocative gesture might serve to discourage an undesired response.

One teacher told how she would give a youngster an assignment, then, before the student even had time to do much more than write their name on the worksheet, she would walk by their desk and write "Great Job!" at the top of their paper. Then, without a word, she'd walk on.

This would bring a puzzled look and a comment like, "Miss, you wrote 'Great Job' on my paper!"

"Uh, yes I did," she would reply.

"But I ain't *done* nothin' yet."

"But don't you intend to do a great job on that worksheet?"

"Well, yeah; but ... "

"There you go." She would smile as she walked on to another student.

Sounds a little *too* easy, doesn't it? She shared that, although this approach will not work with every student, it has worked well for her in improving completion of assigned work and the quality of that work.

What happens when a youngster doesn't fulfill the comments written on their paper? "Simple," she said. "I just pass their desk for a few days and write the comments on other papers instead. Things usually change the second time around."

And here's something really wild! She occasionally puts actual grades on the paper while a youngster is still working on it. Results: She shares that most students will put out extra effort to earn a high grade written on their paper.

If this approach doesn't bring the sort of results you expect with a youngster after a couple of tries, discontinue it. It's a good-faith gesture, but it will not work with everyone.

A Special Education teacher shared this idea at a program at Arizona State University. I did not get her name.

#64

"Don't go there!" hat

Sometimes you just want students to sit in their seats and work quietly until the period is over. Provided you don't overuse this approach, here's an effective way to give students a subtle message, but without having to say anything.

This one came from my wife's cousin, who used to teach elementary school. If she wanted youngsters to work on an assignment at their desks and not interrupt her, she would put on an awful-looking hat. It was so ridiculous that no youngster would forget what it meant.

My wife's cousin is Ann Smelley, of Pleasanton, Texas. Today Ann is the head librarian at Pleasanton High School.

#65

Reclaiming instructional moments

We have only so much time and resources, so isn't it interesting how a few youngsters will try to capture just about all of them (plus your sanity to boot)?

105

It works like this: You put everyone to task, only to have one student camp out at the sharpener. He's grinding the life out of a perfectly healthy #2 pencil, and, when it's down to nubbins, he pulls a fresh one from his jeans and reduces *it* to sawdust.

This could go on forever!

Here we have a moment of truth; there are basically three things you can do:

1. You could ignore him (yeah, right).

2. You could give him the dickens to try to redirect him to task. Two problems here: First, it might not work. Second, considering that there are only so many instructional moments available, the rest of the class pays the price of having less of *you* while your time, energy, and focus are directed toward the pencil sharpener.

3. You could direct your attention to the compliant ones, the rest of the class.

Number 3 might increase your lifespan within the profession. It will also send the pencil grinder a pretty stiff message, but without the hassle. Here's one way to do it (addressing the class while ignoring the one at the sharpener):

You know, class, it's been a pretty grueling day. I'll admit I've worked you pretty hard, and I really appreciate the way you have remained in your seats. So I'm going to give a five-minute bubblegum break to all of you who are in your seats right now, and Mary here is going to help me pass out some sugarless gum (although you could give stickers, pretzels, coupons, sugarless candy, whatever).

Now the one at the pencil sharpener knows he's been had—left out of the deal. You could handle this in one of two ways. First, you could continue to ignore him while adding a postscript for the rest of the class:

> *And I promise you we're going to do this again sometime during this class period tomorrow.*

There's a good chance this youngster doesn't want to get "caught" on the second day.

The other way would be to talk to this youngster frankly:

> *Hey, I'll bet you're thinking that I deliberately waited until you were out of your seat to reward them for being in their seats, huh?*

> *Well, that's right, I did. It was sort of a trick on you, I guess. But I'll tell you what (whispering): I'm going to do the bubblegum thing again tomorrow.*

Of course this kid thinks that you're still up to tricks the next day. He figures the instant his fanny leaves his seat by even six inches, you're going to pull the bubblegum number for those *in* their seats. For that reason, I'd work at cutting him in on the deal simply because he might not expect it. Better yet, I'd find a way to get him *out* of his seat (send him on a short errand), then offer the "deal" when he returns to his seat. With few words there's a clear message: *Tricks are over; enjoy.*

This approach works best with those youngsters whose noncompliant behaviors are fairly mild. It will not work with the more behaviorally difficult youngster who is dead set on hooking you into a conflict. Also, too much reliance on this one approach could render it useless.

This idea comes from *It Makes a Difference* by James D. Sutton (Friendly Oaks Publications, 1990).

#66

Ticket, please

During an assignment, walk through your class, giving a ticket to all youngsters who are on task. At the end of the class let them deposit half of their ticket into a container, keeping the other half as a receipt. Then, after a few days, or at the end of the week, have a drawing for a prize. Suggestion: Make the prize something that will encourage them academically, such as a homework pass (they can get credit for the homework by simply putting the correct heading on their paper and attaching the pass) or an opportunity to drop their lowest daily grade.

It is important that youngsters keep their ticket stubs and be able to produce them later. This in essence fosters skills of responsibility and organization. Also, the opportunity for a youngster to know that he or she is in the drawing is encouraging. Every student who is eligible for the drawing has already won the benefits of their compliance.

This idea is based on one shared by Rebecca Bagley, an eighth-grade teacher in Richmond, Utah.

#67

Jumper cables

During a program once I asked a group of educators, "What bothers you the most about the behavior of oppositional and defiant students?"

"Jumper cables," one teacher replied. "I wish I could just go up to them with a huge battery and jump-start them to tasks."

What a terrific idea. No, not the electrocution of students, but the idea of a visual aid that would, in a fun sort of way, signal the need to get back to task.

Get a large box, paint it black, and write on it something like "Jolt-O Battery Company—Super Student Starter." Attach some battery cables, and put the whole thing on a rolling cart.

Stash the Super Student Starter in a closet or cover it with a blanket until one of those days when tasks grow heavy and patience grows thin. Pull the Super Student Starter down a row of desks and ask, "All right, who needs a jump-start?"

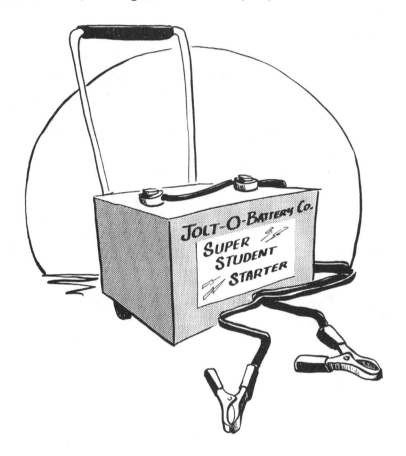

This is bound to get a rise out of them. Depending upon the age of the youngsters, they are apt to either immediately raise their hands or simply laugh. Of course there is no shock (you could experiment on yourself first), but it can be a real hoot for students to pretend that they are jump-starting back to task. After all, redirection back to task is the whole point of this activity, but you are using a fun and creative way to accomplish it.

The unidentified teacher who spoke of jump-starting her students attended my program at region XI Education Service Center in Fort Worth, Texas.

#68

Pencil nap

Here's a power nap—for a pencil. The purpose of this activity is to temporarily break up long periods of sustained attention to a task, especially if it is a difficult one. Of course, this "nap" is actually a break for the students, but it is accomplished in a fun and creative way. Goal: Youngsters will stay focused on the task until "naptime," knowing that their break *will* come.

Run off copies of the sleeping bag, letting each student decorate them to their taste. These can be made out of paper, cloth, felt, plastic, or whatever material is available. The sleeping bags can then be sewn, glued, taped, or stapled. You should do one also.

To initiate the activity, simply shout "Naptime!" to indicate the pencil nap. Each student (and the teacher too) then slips their pencil into the sleeping bag. Set a timer to go off in two to five minutes, indicating when the nap is over. Then it's back to task.

Encourage youngsters to either rest briefly or visit quietly while their pencils nap, careful not to wake them.

Oh yeah, this same activity works well for pens also.

#69

The "Good Medicine" Plan

I am sold on the benefits of empowering youngsters. What they can monitor and change for themselves not only teaches responsibility, it reduces the "hassle factor" considerably. To this end, encourage your students to join you in the "Good Medicine" Plan.

This plan simply means that, when any person takes their "medicine" (responds to gentle

Here's the pattern for the pencil sleeping bag. Cut two pieces this size. Fold the top one down about a third, then tape, staple, glue, or sew the two pieces together.

nonverbal redirection), the consequences will be more favorable for them (milder, less distracting, less embarrassing). Part of the

111

beauty of this approach is that it extends respect, regard, and a sense of reasonableness to a youngster, but without having to say it in words.

Here's how I would teach the "Good Medicine" concept, of course modifying the language and approach for the age and maturity level of the students:

Why do we take medicine sometimes?

(To help us get well when we are sick.)

Is it important to take the medicine?

(Yes, if you want to get well.)

But what if the medicine really tastes awful, and I don't like it?

(You should take it anyway.)

But why? I don't like it.

(Because it is better to take a medicine that tastes bad than to stay sick.)

I'm going to pass out some "Good Medicine" cards. They are sort of like medicine, in a way. If I find that you are not doing your work, or you are keeping someone else from doing their work, I'd first rather give you a little "medicine" (hold up a large, empty medicine bottle and several plastic spoons) *than have to make a big deal out of what you are doing wrong. That might embarrass you, and still not work as well as the "medicine."*

What is this medicine really? It's a hint, that's all—a hint without words. When I place one of these little plastic spoons on your desk it means, "Please get back to work." If you can take that medicine and get back to work, that's it. It doesn't have to go any further than that. Would you agree that taking this small bit of medicine would be the best way for you, for me, and for your classmates?

Pause to let them respond.

It's important that I make this your choice. How many of you want to be on "The 'Good Medicine' Plan" with me?

Peer pressure alone might get the class to follow along, but it is critical to emphasize that this plan is a matter of choice. Any youngster not on the plan will receive traditional, verbal redirection.

You will notice that I have already signed every one of these "Good Medicine" cards. Read it carefully first, then, if any of you want to be part of this plan, sign it also. Put it in the upper left-hand corner of your desk. Anyone who has a card on their desk, and follows what it says, will receive only good medicine from me. That's a promise, and I will keep that promise.

Here's a suggestion for what to put on the card:

I think "The 'Good Medicine' Plan" is a good idea. I want to be part of it."

At this point it might be helpful to role-play how this will work. Answer any questions, being certain to address any potential problems before the plan is put into motion. For instance, one question might be, "How many times in one class period can a person be given a spoon?"

Although a number of things will need to be worked out, the benefits of "The 'Good Medicine' Plan" should be clearly identifiable:

1. The need for excessive verbal redirection is reduced, making the learning environment more beneficial and less distracting to all.

2. It minimizes the sort of conflict with a youngster that might come as a result of verbal redirection.

114

3. It is a challenge that is fun.

4. It empowers through choice; a child does not have to "buy in" to the plan.

5. It teaches a valuable life lesson: sometimes it's best just to "take your medicine."

6. Either way (no redirection needed or the child responded appropriately to redirection), the plan offers an opportunity for affirmation.

Note: In putting the "Good Medicine" Plan together, I began to do a lot of spin-off thinking. For instance, could you offer some incentive to those youngsters who are on the plan, but have required no redirection at all? Be creative; there's plenty of room to build on this strategy.

#70

Stand in the circle

This strategy follows the concept behind "The 'Good Medicine' Plan." Its focus is redirection, not the negativity of consequences (punishment). There *is* a difference.

A circle approximately the size of a Hula Hoop is drawn on the floor (or, for that matter, you could fasten a real Hula Hoop to the floor). Youngsters are instructed that anyone who is off task will be asked to stand in the circle.

"But how long do we have to stand there?" comes the question. Here's a good answer:

> *Oh, it doesn't matter to me. Feel free to step out of the circle whenever you're ready to go back to work. That's all I want.*

Youngsters learn quickly that they can step into the circle, then immediately step out of it and return to their desk. Again, the goal here is redirection rather than punishment.

This creative redirection idea comes from Bobby Doyal, now retired from teaching. He operated the Alternative Education Program for Brady ISD in Brady, Texas.

#71

Time tab

This approach is similar to "Stand in the circle," only more subtle. It works best for the youngster who accepts the concept and terms of "The 'Good Medicine' Plan" and is willing to respond to gentle hints. Explain this as an option which will only work with a student who has excellent self-control and strong social skills.

When you find a youngster off task, simply engage a stopwatch and place it on the student's desk. When the youngster realizes that they are "on the clock" and redirects to task, they stop the watch. This consequence is fair and self-enforcing. The student owes you the elapsed time (before or after school or at lunch or recess—on *their* time). Let the youngster administer the "payment," knowing that they are free to leave after they settle their time tab.

Again, promote this gesture to students as a sophisticated one, explaining that only those who function at the most mature level can handle it. Obviously not all youngsters are candidates for "Time tab."

#72

The victory call

Cellular telephones now provide even more opportunities for some very creative ways to communicate.

Consider painting a cell phone gold and offering a "Gold Phone Award" to youngsters who have met their goals for the week. Deliver the phone directly to a young-ster's desk, and let the student call a parent or grandparent to share the good news of their accomplishment.

Make a production out of it; deliver the phone to the student on a satin pillow. Lots of possibilities here.

A principal shared this idea with me. I cannot identify him.

#73

Magic moment coupon

Kids of all ages love magic. Show them a trick, and they'll all ask the same question: "How did you do that?"

You don't have to be a stage magician to do simple magic tricks that will engage curiosity and spark a little action. Go to your school library and pick up a book on magic. Learn a few simple tricks, and practice them until you can do them well. Then, after giving the class an assignment, show them the trick.

Tell the class that those who finish the assignment in the allotted time (and make an acceptable grade on it) will earn a "Magic moment coupon." Later, at a designated time and place, youngsters can learn how to do the trick. Price of admission: the coupon.

Did you notice that this idea "evolves" from #8 back in chapter three?

#74

"I didn't know" insurance

Ever give an assignment, only to have a student or two say they didn't understand it? Ever hear youngsters say they misunderstood and did a different assignment instead, or that they didn't know that the paper was due *this* Friday?

Frustrating.

To deal with this problem, and provide a little insurance against the "I didn't know" plea, have a student (typically the one who would likely have the most difficulty with it) write the assignment for the class on a piece of newsprint or easel paper. Ask the student to draw a line all the way across the paper about one-third of the way from the bottom. The student is to be exact in copying this assignment onto the upper portion of the newsprint. The assignment not only indicates the work that is to be done, it specifies acceptable completion and notes specifically *when*, *where*, and *how* it is to be turned in.

Compliment the student when he or she finishes posting the assignment. Put your initials in the space below the line, explaining that you are "certifying" the assignment. Explain that this means that you are bound by the terms of the assignment, which means that you cannot make it longer, or more difficult, or expect them to turn it in sooner. You have entered into a binding contract with them.

Ask the student who copied the assignment if he or she now understands it. If they do, ask them to "certify" by putting their initials on the paper with yours.

Next ask the whole class if they understand about the assignment. If they say "yes," ask them come up to the easel and put their initials in the bottom section with yours and the student's, signifying that they understand the assignment, how it is to be handled, and that they are accountable for it.

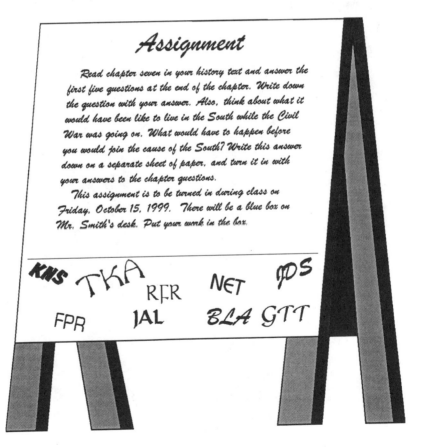

If anyone is still seated, or indicates that they don't understand the assignment, explain it to them until they also can add their initials to the paper. Tape this sheet to the wall in a prominent place, and leave it there until after the assignment is to be turned in.

Now, this approach won't turn everyone into wonder-students, but it will hopefully reduce complaining and excuse-making. It also teaches a lesson on what it means to "seal a deal" with your name or initials.

#75

Classroom refrigerator

This is simply a modification of the home refrigerator, that great showplace of family pride. When my kids were small we never needed two refrigerators, but there were times when we could have used two doors!

For the classroom, make a likeness of a huge refrigerator or just a refrigerator door. One way is to use corkboard squares, gluing them to plywood that has been cut out to shape. Even more creative would be to nail sheet metal to the plywood. That way you could use actual refrigerator magnets instead of push-pins or thumbtacks. Paint the classroom refrigerator and discuss with the class how it will be used.

#76

Self-evaluate

Here's an approach that reaffirms that most youngsters can do an excellent job of evaluating their own work. All they need is the opportunity.

One teacher shared how she would paper-clip a sticker (one her students would want to keep) to the upper right-hand corner of a worksheet. She stapled a small sheet of paper containing a three-item checklist to the upper left-hand corner of the same sheet. The three checklist items were:

- **I finished this worksheet.**
- **I remained in my seat.**
- **I allowed my classmates to finish their work.**

There was only one rule: Any youngster who could check all three items could keep the sticker.

The teacher shared that this idea worked very well. Few youngsters ever abused it, and many of them later shared with her how empowering it was to evaluate their own work and behavior.

Older youngsters won't be too excited about the stickers, so think of other things you could use, such as a coupon for five minutes of free time on Friday.

A teacher from Missouri shared this valuable idea during a program in Columbia. Unfortunately, I did not get her name.

Chapter Six

Like the Working World

Give 'em the business

Sometimes it seems that school and the working world are on different planets. Everything we do in education should be geared to help youngsters make it when they walk out into the "real world." And yet how often do we actually prepare them for the remaining 75% of their lives? Good question.

The business world cries out for young people who can work in a team and think and dream creatively. Even if there's a "not hiring" sign in the store window, most businesses will tell you there's always an opening for the *right* person.

This chapter focuses on a few principles that are *right*, and they're *right* for teaching. Besides, this stuff can be a load of fun (dare we say that too loudly?).

Granted, not all students are going to become millionaires or successful entrepreneurs. They can, however, learn to market their greatest capital asset—themselves.

Five principles of economic success

We're using the word "economic" because it has far-reaching implications. It could mean business or corporate success, other aspects of the world of work, or personal economics. All are applicable, although the main emphasis here is business-oriented.

Principle #1: The ability to work with others

Folks who can get along with others, especially when times are tough, have a way of rising to the top. Knowledge and job skills are important, but there's nothing to replace the skill of effective interaction with others. Put another way, all the job skills in the world will do little to help a person who is indifferent, insensitive, and abrasive.

Principle #2: A philosophy of service

Ultimately everyone is in the service business. It might not appear that way, but, in the end, you'll find service (or, unfortunately, a lack of it). Take the purchase of a new automobile, for example. Although a car seems like a product rather than a service, folks buy automobiles because they want to go from one place to another safely and dependably. That is service.

When folks grasp the service principle, it changes everything. We don't work for wages (and anyone who believes they do will always be broke). We serve, and we are compensated for that service. More service, more compensation. It's not that difficult to become a millionaire, so long as you figure out how to provide a million dollars' worth of service. Seriously, it's being done all the time.

Another component to a philosophy of service is the concept of "and something else." This is the little bit extra that creates the difference between making a living and making a fortune. It's the thirteenth donut in the baker's dozen. It's the extra mile and the reason for cross-training.

I have a friend who underwent extensive dental work that left him feeling uncomfortable for several days. His dentist sent him flowers. My friend was touched and impressed. Smart dentist; he has a patient for life, plus a steady stream of referrals.

And there are plenty of examples of businesses and folks who are quick to say "It's not *my* job." This can look bad to a customer who wants to conduct business. Recently I stayed at a well-known hotel chain, and I noticed a customer had placed a room service tray in the hall outside the door to their room. It had leftover portions of food on it. For nearly three days that tray sat there, even though housekeeping staff and maintenance workers passed by it, and even bumped into it occasionally. (Right; I should have taken it over to the kitchen myself, but I wanted to see how long this would go on.) Sometimes "and something else" means doing a small task, not because it's part of one's regular job, but because it is the right thing to do. Besides, customers *do* notice these things, and it's the customer who ultimately pays the salaries and the bills.

Although I believe "and something else" can be taught, its strongest impact is taught through modeling.

Principle #3: The ability to solve problems

Providing service and solving problems are interrelated. One involves the other. Good salespeople know they don't sell products; they solve the customer's problems. Zig Ziglar is known best for his thoughts on this: "You can have everything in life you want, if you will just help enough other people get what *they* want." True, of course. If they didn't need what you have, they wouldn't have a problem. And if they could have solved the problem without your help, they would have done it already.

The really good news is that problem-solving and critical, solutions-oriented thinking can be taught.

Principle #4: A willingness to take a risk

Those who insist on "playing it safe" will always be playing on someone else's turf. The world is open to those who are willing to take a risk. I tell young people that, if they can handle risk, they will win on one, maybe two, counts. First of all, they might achieve what they risk for. Second, and even more important, they absolutely will win the battle over indecision and fear of risking.

It needs to be clear that we are talking about *appropriate* risks. Every youngster knows that, in order to participate in group sports, they must deal with the thought of losing a game or a season. This kind of appropriate risk stands in sharp contrast to foolhardy risks (such as playing "chicken" with traffic). Youngsters who take foolhardy risks, especially with their lives, aren't demonstrating their courage—they're displaying their stupidity! And isn't it interesting how youngsters who will take foolhardy risks usually *won't* take appropriate risks?

Principle #5: The ability to implement and follow a plan

There's a good reason that we don't teach much regarding the skills of goal-setting. It's because we don't do it very well ourselves. Whether it's personal goal-setting or the work of a group, the ability to develop a plan and follow it is critical. Only when a plan is clearly conceptualized, broken down into achievable objectives, and acted upon do we have something to evaluate afterward.

No responsible business would open shop without a business plan. Why should a classroom project be any different?

Teaching the principles

Share the five principles of economic success with the students. We've turned this into a question-and-answer sort of activity. Be aware, however, that many of these questions and concepts could easily be channeled into brainstorming activities. Also, note that these next two activities can be done with an entire class or with the class working in groups.

#77

The first three principles

This activity addresses the first three principles: ability to work with others, a philosophy of service, and problem-solving. The questions and directions here are only suggestions. Feel free to expand upon them.

> *Class, when we study what makes businesses succeed, we can better learn how we can be prepared to do well for ourselves in a working world. In fact, we will even do some "business" kinds of activities to help us learn the principles.*

> *There are five principles; let's discuss them* (it would be helpful to put the five on the blackboard or overhead). *The first principle is the ability to get along with others. Do you agree with that? Why would that be so important?*

At this point you might break the class into groups and ask each group to come up with at least three reasons that it is important for those in business together to get along.

> *Can you think of any businesses that would be in big trouble if the folks didn't get along? How would you know that such a business was beginning to have trouble?*

If they don't bring it up, mention that professional sports are owned and operated as a business—a very clear example of where getting along with one another is critical all the way to the bank!

> *If a business knew they were in trouble because folks were not getting along, how could they fix the problem?*

Is a classroom like this one kind of like a business? In what ways? Is getting along with one another important? Why?

The next principle is a philosophy of service. First of all, what is a "philosophy," and what do we mean by "service"?

If you don't have any takers on the question, offer your own interpretation and go on.

Do you think this principle is important? How could a desire to serve others help someone become successful in their business? What effect would it have on future business?

Now there are "service" businesses. See if your group can think of three service businesses.

You should get responses of everything from running a laundry to the practice of medicine.

Even businesses that we don't think of as being service businesses really do provide some kind of service. Sales is an example. How can a person who sells a product, like an automobile, be providing a service to customers? Can you think of any other businesses that don't sell a service, but are really in the service business?

As we have already mentioned earlier in this chapter, a car salesman, in selling an automobile, provides a service of dependable transportation that will take the customer from where they are to where they want to go. There are similar purposes of service in essentially all aspects of sales. Even a restaurant doesn't just sell food; it handles hunger.

> *Class, another important part of the principle of service is something called "and something else." It means to give more than you have to, or to be able to do more than just one job or task. Why do you think this is important? Can you think of any examples of "and something else"?*

Explain about the baker's dozen and the idea of doing one's job while being able and willing to do all or part of another one also, if necessary.

> *The third principle is the ability to solve problems. How would this ability help someone who is in business to serve others?*

You should have some good discussion here, especially considering that many service businesses exist to solve problems. Some examples include TV, computer, and automobile repair.

> *Zig Ziglar, a man who has trained thousands of folks in sales, is well known for saying, "You can have everything in life you want, if you will just help enough other people get what they want." What would it mean to a person who seriously followed his advice?*

#78

The last two principles

The focus here is on risk-taking and planning.

Class, the fourth principle says that one must be willing to take a risk. Exactly what does it mean to take a risk?

There are good risks and there are bad risks that are inappropriate. What would be some examples of each? How can we learn to tell a good risk from a bad risk? Does the sort of risk a person takes, good or bad, say something about them? What does it say?

If a person is unwilling to take even a good risk, how might that affect them in business? Can you think of some examples, or even folks you know, who took a good business risk, and it worked out well for them?

And the last principle mentions the ability to develop a plan and follow it. Someone once said, "If you fail to plan, you are planning to fail." What does that mean?

Now, not many of you are in business just yet, but have you or your family ever had to plan something? How does it help to have a plan?

Weddings, vacations, moving, and even funerals are some possible examples.

When we make plans for our own lives, it is called goal-setting. Setting goals helps us to know the steps we have to take to reach our goals. When we put time frames on these goals we become aware of our progress toward them. It's important to put priorities on goals, because some are more important than others. And it's also important to have some goals we can reach fairly quickly, as well as goals that will take some time, even five or ten years. Then, when we reach a goal—it's time to celebrate! How many of you like to celebrate?

Show your students the Goals Worksheet, or run it off and give them a copy of it. Working on personal goals could obviously be a very comprehensive activity of its own.

Folks develop business plans which help them determine the goals for a new business they want to open. Planning is very important for success in business. We will be doing some thinking and planning activities as we continue to study economic success.

Goals Worksheet

Personal Habits/Characteristics:

Health/Physical:

Career:

Financial/Property:

Educational/Learning:

Recreation:

Home/Family:

Social:

Spiritual:

Other:

The Goals Worksheet, as well as a process for individual goal-setting, is covered in Chapter 17 of *If My Kid's So Nice ... Why's He Driving ME Crazy?* by Dr. James Sutton (Friendly Oaks Publications, 1997). The Goals Worksheet is reprinted here with permission.

Applying the principles

Here are some activities that provide the opportunity for students to apply the principles they have learned.

#79

Brew up a brainstorm

Brainstorming as a strategy for collecting ideas is not a new concept; it's been around awhile. The process makes an exciting activity for those who have never experienced it.

The corporate world, especially in those business applications that succeed or fail on the availability of new and fresh ideas (such as advertising and product development), relies on brainstorming to collect a "pool" of material for consideration and development.

Although I have been a part of brainstorming groups on many occasions, I continue to be amazed at the power and "team-ness" of this simple process. The effectiveness of brainstorming was again demonstrated to me recently at a chapter meeting of the National Speakers Association. Members were to give rapid-fire suggestions for topics of future programs; there was a 90-second time limit. Over 30 topics were suggested, most of them viable and on-target. No questionnaires, no mailings, no postage, and no hassle—in 90 seconds! Impressive.

What makes brainstorming work is the fact that it is time-limited. Participants know that it is not going to drag on forever. The objective is clearly stated:

> *When I say go, I want you to come up with as many uses for a newspaper (for example) as you can think of in one minute. We're not going to evaluate any of your suggestions at this time. We just want to collect as many uses as we can in the time allowed. Ready, go!*

Brainstorming requires a timekeeper and at least two scribes, with each scribe recording every other idea or suggestion. Three might be even better, with each scribe recording every third suggestion; this frees the class to go as quickly as they want. That way, nothing is lost. Have the scribes read all of the suggestions to the class, and praise them for their efforts. Let them know that brainstorming gets even better with practice.

Conclude this process by again sharing with your students that this is one way that multi-million-dollar companies stay ahead of their competition. The wealth of a company is *not* in a bank; it's in the minds and the creativity of its employees. If your students have difficulty accepting this idea, have them consider the cost of massive computer software programs. Is the expense in the floppy disks or the one or two CDs that rest inside the colorful box? Hardly; the consumer pays for the brainpower that was put onto those CDs. Ideas are eternal; they can be created, but they can never be destroyed.

A number of activities throughout this book discuss using this brainstorming procedure to develop material. This is an excellent way to use one activity to create another.

Consider brainchains. Here's a challenging and visual way for youngsters to engage in a little healthy competition, as well as an easy way to keep score of ideas. Break the class into groups as they begin a brainstorming session. Have the scribes in each

133

group write the contributed ideas on strips of paper. The strips are then made into paper chains—brainchains. See which group has the longest chain when the bell sounds.

#80

Mindmapping

When your class becomes proficient at brainstorming, try mindmapping. Mindmapping is a way of organizing the thoughts, ideas, and suggestions that are collected. Mindmapping makes it easy to group concepts and ideas for study and action.

Brainstorming is linear; one idea follows another. And when the ideas are written down on a piece of paper, they are written in columns. It's very similar to playing songs on an audio cassette. As long as the tape is playing, it is going to take the songs in order. It's going to be the same order every time, no exceptions. The songs are "stuck" that way on the cassette; you're not going to change them or their order.

But did you ever make a list of some sort, then realize that you had to insert another item between two others, messing up your neat list (or making you rewrite it)? That's a drawback of linear processing.

If brainstorming is like playing a cassette tape, then mindmapping is like playing a CD, a compact disk. A CD doesn't have to follow a linear pattern of play; you can put the machine on "shuffle," and it will mix up the songs all day long. Mindmapping is visualized more like the spokes of a wheel, which are connected to yet more wheels and more spokes, instead of a column of data. It could also be visualized as branching, as in the diagramming of sentences (your favorite task in junior high English, right?). Mindmapping's power and application are especially realized in large projects that have many parts and subparts. In this way everything stays connected and organized, but there is plenty of room for creativity. Authors use mindmapping to get the "whole picture" of the book they are writing. I know; I used it in writing this book.

For purposes of practicing these concepts in your classroom, do a brainstorming activity, then organize the collected material using mindmapping. Brainchains could be mindmapped by grouping the ideas collected into their own subchains coming off the main brainchain. Let the groups be creative in how they structure this. After all, if it works, it works.

#81

Here's my card

Here's an activity that quickly connects with the world of business and commerce—a business card. In this activity students learn about business cards and how to use them. As a bonus, each youngster is affirmed by this activity, and the concept of team (the class or group) is also reinforced.

Mary Smith

Mrs. Blackburn's History Class   Sidell Avenue Intermediate School
                                                                  Anywhere, USA

135

Although it would be a fun activity for each youngster to make his or her own business card, I believe that the activity will have more impact if you surprise the class with them.

There are a number of software programs around for making business cards on a computer (it can even be done with a drawing program). The only thing that has to be individualized on each card would be the student's name. Ink jet printers will make the best-quality cards, although they could be run off in sheets on a copier, then cut on a paper cutter.

One way to introduce the cards would be to place only ten cards on each student's desk before class starts. As class begins, ask them if they know of any adults who have business cards. Why do they have them? Show them the international protocol for presenting business cards. Discuss why each part of the protocol is important; then let them practice presenting cards to each other.

Let the class use their creativity and artistic ability to fashion a card holder for their cards (you could either tie this into an art activity, or cross-teach with the art teacher).

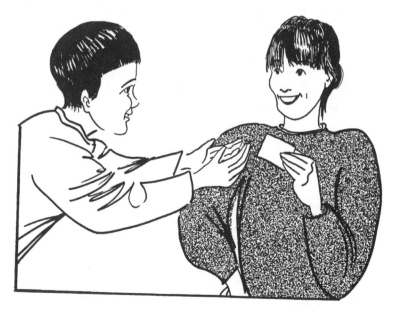

Give them an assignment with their new cards. Tell them that they must give away all ten of their cards (tell them you will be giving them more) using the international protocol. But there's one catch: At least five of the cards must be given to someone other than a classmate. It might be fun for a youngster to ask for a card from an adult who they know carries them, so that they will have an opportunity to practice receiving cards. Give them a deadline for the assignment, and provide an opportunity for them to share their experiences of card giving and receiving. Don't forget to replenish their supply.

How to Exchange Business Cards

International protocol and ethics

---

1. Information on your card should clearly explain who you are. It should be easy to read. If you are in another country, one side of the card should be printed in the language of the host. Note: The printing or embossing of both sides of the card should be of equal quality.

2. Practice presenting and receiving business cards with both hands (especially when you are in Asia). Exception: In Moslem Asia or the Middle East, use only the right hand (the left hand is considered unclean).

3. When you receive a card, do not put it away quickly. Study it, and use it to create conversation. Put the card in your card case when the other person puts your card away.

4. Never scribble or write notes on another person's card for any reason.

5. Always carry cards in a high-quality business card case.

Thanks to Marie Betts-Johnson of Rancho Santa Fe, California, for these business card tips. Marie is president of the International Business Protocol Institute.

#82

Class logo

Develop something that brings the class together as a unit. Where possible, use brainstorming to do it. Suggestions could include a class shield or flag. Everyone can work on these, and they can be displayed in the classroom.

Another idea might be a class logo on a cloth patch, which students could wear on their clothing or put on their backpacks. The logo patch could even be made into adhesive stickers (photo places and novelty businesses can make inexpensive photo stickers) and placed on bookcovers. Let the class use their creativity and imagination on this one. Perhaps you could have a logo contest, with some sort of prize for the winner. Check out the last chapter of this book if you need to raise some money to fund such a project.

A similar idea would be for the class to design and produce a class tee-shirt. This tee-shirt concept could also be part of a fundraising venture, especially if it is associated with a benevolent project (such as a sponsorship or adoption, as covered in the next chapter).

How about a class quilt, with each youngster bringing a piece for the quilt? What a special way this would be to include every youngster as a part of a significant effort. Enlist parents and grandparents to help with the quilt. The quilt could be raffled to fund a benevolent project.

Remember, these ideas are just to get you started. Your best resources for ideas are your students and their families.

#83

Communication Central

Communication is essential within any business or corporation. Without it, chaos and confusion will consume the best of plans. There are two components to communication, inside (for use within the organization) and outside (to be shared outside the organization). Both have a vital role in maintaining the health of the organization.

If you don't have one already, develop a message center for your classroom so that expectations, plans, and the responsibilities that students have to you and each other can be posted and monitored. This could be a part of the bulletin board or even an extension of some ideas and activities that have already been discussed in other parts of this book (see #74, for example).

Inside communication is important within the corporate and business world whether the news is posted next to the water cooler or is e-mailed. Inside communication could be accomplished at school through a weekly classroom newsletter. The students can help with it, and everyone is expected to read it—and heed it.

Outside communication lets the rest of the school and the community know about your class and its contributions and projects. This might come naturally as newspapers and radio stations want to learn more about what you are doing, or it might be something that is sent to the news media, such a press release or article. Think about this sort of communication when you begin to approach sponsors for your projects. And what about a web site built and maintained by your class?

Keep in mind that it is important to clear all outside communication with your administrator. They shouldn't learn of your activities through another source.

#84

A classroom "business"

What good would it do to have a chapter on business application of classroom skills if we didn't include some ideas for creating a business in the classrooom? Such a project provides a vivid impression of how all skills, principles, communication, and processes come together in the medium of free enterprise.

Of course you can use your brainstorming process for arriving at an appropriate business venture, but here are a few that came to my mind as I was wrapping up this chapter:

- What about that backpack sticker idea from chapter four (#34)? It might have some really great possibilities.

- Consider the handmade paper idea from chapter five (#50).

- Design and sell tee-shirts or bumper stickers. This could be strictly to raise funds, or they could be used to promote a class project.

- Make and sell lapel buttons. They are cheap to produce, and now with digital cameras and printers, it's easy to put a person's picture on the button. Of course, buttons can also be used to publicize important projects.

- How about putting together a class cookbook? It could be of the serious variety (using recipes of parents and grandparents) or a humorous cookbook (just imagine the recipes that kindergartners can dream up).

While doing some training for a BOCES in Wyoming, I heard of a small school district in South Dakota that encouraged youngsters to individually develop some sort of marketable business while in high school. Although I was unable to contact the school, the concept is an excellent one. There are probably other high schools around the country doing this.

Chapter Seven

Sponsorships and Adoptions

Going to the dogs ... and other animals

This chapter extends the notion of service that was introduced in the last chapter. It reflects the responsibility we all have to make our world a better place for those living in it. Sensitivity and responsibility to others and to the environment is a valued attribute that should be nourished in our young people.

We start with sponsorships and adoptions of animals.

#85

Sponsor a homeless pet

I once read about a woman who would spend most of her lunch hour at an animal shelter walking the dogs. The dogs seemed to appreciate this attention and exercise. And, whenever one of them was adopted, they were easier to handle. I'm sure a lot of the dogs were glad to see her come around.

Although I'm not suggesting that your class go out and walk dogs, it might make an excellent project for a class to sponsor a dog or cat at a shelter. For the sake of the animal and the class, it is important that you have the assurance that, regardless of whether it is actually adopted, the animal will remain alive ("no-kill" animal shelters, those that will not destroy any of the animals so long as there are room and donations and support for them, are on the rise).

Explain to the class that many of the dogs and cats at these shelters are, like people sometimes, victims of circumstance. They belonged to families who loved them, but could no longer care for them or take them along on a move. The nearest large town to my office, San Antonio, has a large number of shelters for animals because it is a military town. Families move often, and cannot always take their pets with them.

If a class decides to support a dog or a cat (or even one of each), take photos of the animal and put them up in a special place in the class. Make the animal real to the students by explaining as much of the circumstances as possible, including the pet's name, if it is known. Determine what it would take to support the animal's care each month, and present it to the class as an opportunity and a challenge. Decide if the class wants to raise the money in some way (bringing in aluminum cans, for instance), or if each student will simply donate to the pet's care. One dollar per month per student should take care of something like this. Consider writing a note to the parents of your students explaining the project, and the important things that are to be learned by it.

If it could be worked out, it might be helpful to let the dog or cat come to the school for a visit. There's nothing like having a look at the real thing to remind a youngster about their adoption project.

If the animal shelter will allow it, put a small sign at the animal's pen, reading something like: "Sparky's care is being supported by Mrs. Johnson's fourth-grade class at Newton Elementary School." Get publicity on this within the community; other schools and classes might do the same.

To incorporate this project into academic activity, have the students write letters to Sparky (older youngsters might prefer to write to the shelter). Encourage the shelter to write back, commenting on the animal's care and the thoughtfulness of the class. Have a small celebration whenever the pet is adopted permanently; then select another animal to sponsor.

Consider a sign-up sheet for weekends and after school for those youngsters who want to visit the pet at the shelter and exercise the animal. Take a few moments on Monday morning in class for youngsters to share about their visit with the adopted pet.

One potential problem might come up when every tender-hearted kid in your class wants to adopt the pet themselves. Of course, adoption is the whole point, but it does seem important to take a little time so that a classmate is certain that they want to raise the animal as their own. Consider some sort of adoption process, including making a certain number of visits to the animal at the shelter.

As a supplement to the idea of adopting a pet at the animal shelter, I want to stress the value of using animals in working with shy or resistant youngsters. They just have a way of getting through where we can't. One counselor shared with me that she was having a problem getting a youngster to talk to her. I suggested that she take him to a store and let him pick out a leash, then take him to an animal shelter and let him walk a dog. It worked.

#86

Sponsor an animal at the zoo

Your class might not be able to take a cheetah for a walk, but the rest of the idea's basically the same.

Reaching out to others

These ideas for sponsorships and adoptions benefit other people.

#87

Sponsor a third world child

There are a number of "Help the Children" types of programs around. These programs allow an individual to sponsor the needs and education of a youngster who would otherwise go without. Why not support a third world child as a class?

The advantage of this kind of sponsorship is that your class can identify with the child, especially if the selected youngster is close to their own age. There's even the opportunity for communication with the child through letters and photographs. The one main disadvantage is that your students will likely never have any direct contact with the child they support.

Thanks go to my pastor's daughter, Jolee Woodward of Pleasanton, Texas, for this idea. Jolee and her college roommate contribute monthly to the care of a six-year-old in Brazil. Part of the proceeds from this book will go to do the same.

#88

Adopt a senior citizen or a shut-in

Put out a call to churches, individuals, and agencies within the community to identify an elderly person who lives alone and could use some help (if the class tries to adopt one person in a nursing home, there is bound to be some jealousy from those who were not adopted). Consider things that your class and their families can do for this person, from yardwork to taking them to the grocery store.

What an opportunity for your students to visit, write, and call this person, and to follow the seasons of the year with cards, handmade gifts, and lots of thoughtfulness! This activity is made even more special in that many of your students might not have close access to their own grandparents and great-grandparents. This project allows them that kind of contact.

#89

Adopt a nursing home

This idea is similar to helping a senior citizen, except that it is for the whole nursing home and those who live there. Just about all of the folks there can use some help reading or writing letters, or just having someone to visit with them for a while.

Perhaps your class could plan some special events or programs at the nursing home, especially during Christmas season and other holidays. Parents of your students could even offer to drive someone to the doctor, or pick up a prescription or an item from the store. There are lots of possibilities here. Use the brainstorming process to generate ways the class could be of service.

#90

Adopt the school custodian

For a week, have your class adopt the school's custodian (also called the janitor). After all, who's the hardest-working person on the campus?

I've seen this done to everyone's delight. One group of youngsters arranged to adopt the custodian for a week. They borrowed a key to the custodian's closet, and, when the custodian was away, they left surprises among the brooms and mopbuckets. When the custodian arrived, there were cards, balloons, flowers and plants, fruit, candy, movie tickets, and desserts awaiting her every day. She was delighted.

It's also possible for a class to do this project anonymously, adding an element of intrigue in trying to surprise the custodian without being discovered.

This is not an original idea. I have heard of schools doing different renditions of this "adopt the custodian" project.

#91

Adopt the school counselor, principal, or secretary

It's the same general idea, only different folks. A week is plenty long enough.

#92

Adopt the school's paraprofessionals

Where would we be without the classroom paraprofessionals, the teacher aides? How about setting aside a week to adopt them?

#93

Adopt the teachers' lounge

Are we treading on hallowed ground here? Hey, it's just a thought. Posters and banners that all say, in one way or another, "We appreciate you!" certainly have a way of making their point. Goodies for a week won't hurt either.

Special Saturday sponsorships and adoptions

These projects involve a group of youngsters on a specific half-day Saturday project away from the school.

#94

Clean up

Are you aware of an eyesore along your drive to work every morning? Is it something that your class could clean up in a half-day special Saturday project? If you do attempt such a project, do not do it too often or for too long. That way, you'll maintain interest and parental support.

Don't forget to take lots of photos before and after the project, and post them on your classroom refrigerator. Why not finish with a hot dog lunch at your house?

#95

Adopt a homeless shelter

When my son Jamie was a child care specialist at a residential treatment facility for young boys he saw a big problem brewing between Christmas and New Year's Day. There was no school, and the time on the boys' hands made them irritable and difficult. The next year the staff decided to take the boys to a homeless shelter during this dreaded week. Not only did the boys help out in some small ways (sweeping, cleaning, packing food baskets), they learned to focus on someone other than themselves. What a benefit!

There are a lot of possibilities here for service, especially during the winter months when folks need the protection of the shelters. Consider also other kinds of seasonal projects that can be of service in the community.

Environmental sponsorships and adoptions

These projects serve the environment and teach a valuable lesson of responsibility to the natural world around us. Of course they also teach the value and pride of a job well done.

#96

Adopt a river, lake, or wetland

Clean-up projects not only enhance the beauty of the rivers, lakes, and wetlands being adopted, they help the fish and fowl who make it their home. And what a powerful lesson for youngsters to learn for a lifetime.

#97
Adopt a park or a wildlife refuge

A very similar idea, just a different place. Just about any city or county park would appreciate a little help, and it might cause students to be more environmentally aware when they go to that park with their families. Again, take lots of pictures.

#98
Adopt a stretch of highway

Many states now let groups and organizations adopt a mile or several miles of the highway to keep clean. Just imagine how exciting it is for a group of kids to clean that stretch of road the first time or two, then how tough it must be to get volunteers to come back regularly. Still, it's another way to serve. And it does make a difference when done faithfully.

Obviously it is important to have plenty of adult supervision when working with youngsters along busy highways.

#99
Sponsor an environmental art contest

Sponsor a contest to see which student or class can come up with the best picture or sculpture, only their art must be made of the trash they have picked up on the way to school, or on the school grounds. Creative, fun, and constructive.

#100
Adopt a bulletin board

If there is a bulletin board (or space for one) on a wall in a high-traffic area at your school, consider encouraging your class to adopt it. Many of the activities and projects in this book would make excellent subject matter for such a bulletin board at school. You could title it "How We Are Making a Difference." Be creative; the ideas are endless.

#101

Adopt a garden

If there is a small plot of ground around the school that could use a little sprucing up, let your class take it on as a project. This is an excellent way to teach the necessity of planning and the idea of ensuring a benefit in the future (this ties into several ideas and activities introduced in the last chapter). It's a project that could last all year in some parts of the country. Plants and flowers could be taken from the garden to a nursing home, thus connecting activities and projects. Be certain to include a little sign at the plot explaining the project.

Chapter Eight

Bonus Chapter:
Financing Your Projects

Schools are in the business of education, not fundraising. It's important always to keep this in mind when raising financial support for class or school-wide projects.

Many schools and school districts have specific policies about fundraising, how it is conducted, who can conduct it, and how the money is handled. Still, the very activity of fundraising creates yet another opportunity for youngsters to practice the qualities of significance, teamwork, and spontaneity. Fundraising then becomes not merely a means to an end, but rather a process for a beginning.

A strong corps of adult volunteers can deepen your community contacts and strengthen your efforts. In some cases they can serve as guides and consultants for your class projects. Use them well and often, and everyone will benefit.

By far, however, your richest gold mine for project funding will be your students. After all, who can resist a kid with a mission? And youngsters can get publicity over adults every time.

Bonus #1

The old "tried and true"

Garage sales, bake sales, car washes, and aluminum can drives will always work. So will sales of breakfast tacos, pancake suppers, and spaghetti dinners. If folks gather for a meal (instead of take-out), involve your students as part of the entertainment. This not only will make the evening more enjoyable, it will bring in folks who might not come otherwise.

Bonus #2

Publish a needs list

Lots of folks are willing and eager to help, but they can't read your mind. You must tell them what you want. Write a brief article about your project (with photos, if possible). Always ask for specific things, such as three shovels, four boxes of large trash bags, a dozen tulip bulbs, and four pairs of gloves. The more specific the better, as it will say that you are serious and that you have a plan. Also, it allows folks to contribute something they perhaps already have. Cash is not always the ultimate need, nor do folks always have it to give.

Needs lists can be published in the newspaper, as well as church or community bulletins. It wouldn't be unusual to end up with more than you asked for (what a problem!). Find an adult volunteer who will take the calls and coordinate the collection of items donated. In some places, such as churches, collection boxes can be set out in high-traffic areas. Folks can drop off their items as they come into the building.

Involve your students. Assign them to write thank-you notes, an excellent and practical way to work the project into core academics.

Bonus #3

A shower for the teacher

Here's an idea that turns your needs list into a party of recognition and support. Have a special shower for the teacher, with gifts addressing the needs list.

Consider throwing a shower for a new teacher. Instead of the usual bridal or baby shower gifts, those attending the shower should bring items from the needs list. These gifts could include an easel with newsprint pads, reams of paper, packages of pencils, markers and crayons, scissors, poster board, construction paper, paste, and custom bulletin board materials. Even though most schools furnish these materials to the teachers, supplies are often limited.

Bonus #4

Sponsors

When Hurricane Andrew destroyed the homes and affected the lives of so many folks in Florida and surrounding areas, a prominent entertainer sent relief in the form of an eighteen-wheeler full of pet food. It was a generous and thoughtful gesture.

If your class decides to adopt a homeless pet, perhaps there is a pet food manufacturer or supplier who would agree to help you, receiving valuable exposure in the process. Helping kids and pets is not only good for the kids and pets, it's good press and great for business.

Want to create a garden? Approach a nursery. Want clothing and bedding for the homeless? Approach a department store. Want to clean up an overgrown lot? Approach a hardware store.

Bonus #5

Raffle the class quilt

If your class produces a class quilt (see #82 from chapter six) or some similar product, consider having a raffle for it.

Bonus #6

"Can't refuse" donations

I once received a request for a donation to a cause I knew little about. But I simply could not refuse it. It was from a dear family friend who had known me most of my life. She asked for a nominal donation for her charity. But here was the clincher: All checks were to be addressed to the charity, but mailed to her. She then sent them all in together. Of course there is a little subtle pressure in this tactic, but it *is* effective.

This approach demonstrates one way for a person with a few solid contacts to pull together some powerful support. I've used this approach in my church to encourage a few of the "deeper pockets" to pay the way for kids to go to summer camp. And they loved doing it. Give this approach serious consideration. It might well be a way to raise a considerable amount of support very quickly. Parents and their networks of influence can be a resource just waiting to be tapped.

Bonus #7

Project tee-shirts

If your project is something that lends itself to increased community awareness, consider special tee-shirts that depict the project and encourage support for it. The aim could be the sale of the project tee-shirts directly, or the shirts could be an acknowledgment of a donation.

Bonus #8

Project bumper stickers

This idea is similar to the tee-shirts, only it is a bumper sticker that is sold or given as a "thank-you" for the donation. This is also an excellent way to gain a lot of publicity for the project. More folks are apt to read a bumper sticker than a tee-shirt.

Bonus #9

Sell class recipe books

Recipe books always sell well, and do not need to be expensive to produce. Parents, grandparents, aunts, and uncles of the students can be encouraged to contribute their favorite recipes. Let your students handle this venture as a business project, including the collection of recipes, putting them together with artwork, printing the books, and sales.

An interesting twist on this idea for kindergarten students is to let the students supply the recipes. What creativity. I've seen several of these cookbooks, and they are a hoot!

Bonus #10

Sell "stuff"

A wise elementary school secretary of many years shared with me the secret to successful sales projects for raising funds. She said: "If you can eat it, it'll sell." And she was right. Although there have been excellent products offered for sale, from candles to carnations, candy and snack products *always* do well.

Bonus #11

Store receipts

Some businesses will rebate 1% or more of collected store receipts to the charity that brings them in. It might be worthwhile to approach grocery stores and department stores with this idea. Notify parents of the participating businesses, and encourage them to send their cash register receipts to school. The receipts are then tallied and taken back to their respective businesses, where the school, class, or project is presented with either a check or a voucher for merchandise.

If folks want their receipts back after they are tallied, have them include their name and address on the back.

Bonus #12

Rebates on product labels

A number of food manufacturers offer schools cash or "in kind" contributions for the collection of their products' labels. Although this is not a new idea, it is likely that other manufacturers and suppliers would do the same if they were approached. Never underestimate the buying power and market impact of several hundred youngsters, their families, and their extended families.

Bonus #13

Restaurant proceeds

There is a pizza parlor in my hometown that will donate 10% of your tab to the church of your choice on any Sunday you have lunch or dinner with them. Some restaurants will even donate a percentage of their profits from a designated night. All you have to do is get the word out. You don't have to ask for a cent! Why not involve the youngsters in an after-dinner program (which is about a project, of course). That should bring in the folks. This fundraising idea is a lot of fun, without a lot of work.

Bonus #14

Pre-sell movie tickets

If you have a theater in or near your community, make a deal with them to let you pre-sell movie tickets to friends and family in return for a small commission on each ticket. The generic tickets can then be exchanged for feature tickets at the theater. Everyone wins; the theater picks up a little more business (and *all* the concession stand sales), folks take in a good movie, and your project gets funded. Suggestion: Try to work in an incentive, such as a free soft drink or small popcorn with the pre-sold ticket.

For those folks who would rather have their entertainment at home, the same approach might work with video rentals.

Bonus #15

Coupon cards

My wife buys one of these every year in support of our nephew's soccer team. It costs only a few dollars. We recover the whole expense the very first week or two with the meals, products, and service discounts offered by merchants featured on the card (such as a dollar off on submarine sandwiches, or two dinners for the price of one). These plastic coupon cards can be attractive options for merchants because they don't have to pay anything to participate; they only have to honor their deal when a customer shows them the card.

One company that makes these cards is the Nordis Network. This company can be reached by calling (800) 881-KARD.

Bonus #16

Arts and crafts show

I started an annual arts and crafts show as a fundraising project years ago, and it financed the whole annual budget for child welfare projects. To this day this show supports the needs of many children, and it has become a heralding event of the Christmas season.

Volunteers work like the dickens on this project, but it's over in a day—with a healthy profit! A school would make an excellent location for such an event. Consider it; the rewards and the goodwill can be substantial.

Go to an arts and crafts show near your community. Collect names and addresses of those folks you would like to contact later. Ask around for the names of other folks, and start a data base for your mailing list.

There are individuals who put together newsletters containing information about upcoming arts and crafts shows. Ask around; see if you can contact them, and have them publicize your event in their newsletter. This brings in quality crafters. Many crafters prefer to do the small community events rather than the huge mall extravaganzas.

The simplest way to make money with an arts and crafts show is to charge for booth space. Treat your exhibitors well; they are your Golden Goose. Advertise your event and send flyers home with your students. Encourage folks to stay (and keep buying) by including students in ongoing programs and by having drawings for items donated by the crafters.

We never charged admission to our annual arts and crafts show, but we did set out a large goldfish bowl. It had a sign by it which read: "Thank you for your donations and your support." We raised a considerable amount of cash with this low-key reminder. We also sold snacks, refreshments, and sandwich plates during the show.

Your Turn

When I took on the task of writing this book, I originally titled it *50 Ways to Make Your Classroom Special* as I sat waiting for a flight at DFW Airport. At the time, I was digging hard to come up with even 50 ways. Then, as I looked through my files and became more involved in the project and talked about it with other educators, those 50 expanded into more than enough for this book, and part of another one.

And I am very aware of the fact that the ideas and activities you have read here are just the beginning.

There's an old adage that goes: "The proof of the pudding is in the eating." If the ideas and activities in this book are going to be effective for you, they must be tried, refined, and replicated in *your* setting. So try them.

Please let me hear from you. You can reach me, James D. Sutton, at the address and phone for Friendly Oaks Publications listed on the copyright page and at the end of this book.

If you have ideas and activities you'd like to share with others, contact me with those also. We might include them in an upcoming edition of our newsletter, *Reaching Out*. Or, who knows, we might just put together *another* book. If we print your idea or activity in another book, you'll get an autographed copy of that book with our compliments.

I am also in the process of developing a teacher in-service program that follows the ideas, concepts, and principles covered in this book. It will provide plenty of opportunity for "hands-on" activities and sharing. Any interested schools or school districts can reach me through the Friendly Oaks Publications address and phone.

Ordering This Book

It speaks?

From the beginning of my plans for this book I wanted to get it into the hands of as many teachers as possible. But I didn't necessarily want *them* to have to purchase it.

I'll explain. There was a time when educators were special. The community honored them. They received discounts on clothing, food, and haircuts (at least in the barbershops where I was a regular)—just because they were teachers. It was a status and a privilege they shared with the clergy. With fondest memories of those times, I had an idea, an idea whose partial fruition is in your hands right now—a book that just might be able to speak. With a little help I believe it can say, "Thank you!"

Friendly Oaks Publications and I have agreed to make *101 Ways to Make Your Classroom Special* available at deep discounts to any entity that will make it a gift (a type of premium) to the staff of a school or school district. This could include parent-teacher organizations, a church or synagogue, civic clubs, or a community project. But it could also include a school's or district's vendors. What better way for a bank, food service company, or utility provider to give back to a school or school district that supports them? And, with a little planning, a specific "Thank you!" can be customized on a bookmark to complete the package. Everyone benefits, including the students. Those schools or school districts who prefer to order the book directly for their staff will, of course, also be eligible for the same excellent discounts. Here's the pertinent information for those interested in such a plan:

Teacher Premium Plan
Friendly Oaks Publications
Box 662, Pleasanton, TX 78064
(800) 659-6628
Fax: (830) 281-2617

Orders for single copies

Single copies of this book are also available through the address and phone listed above. Credit cards (Mastercard and Visa) are accepted. The book is $11.95 per copy, plus $4.00 shipping and handling. Orders shipped to addresses in Texas will be charged a state sales tax.

Notes: